Fourth Edition

Introductory
Musicianship

A Workbook

THEODORE A. LYNN

Los Angeles Valley College

Fourth Edition

Introductory

Musicianship

A Workbook

Harcourt Brace Jovanovich College Publishers

Fort Worth   Philadelphia   San Diego   New York   Orlando   Austin   San Antonio
Toronto   Montreal   London   Sydney   Tokyo

Acquisitions Editor: Cindy Kumagawa
Manuscript Editor: Cheryl Hauser
Production Editor: Katherine Watson
Designer: Diana Jean Parks
Art Editor: Elizabeth Banks
Production Manager: Lynne Bush

Cover credit: © Lori Mitchell.

Library of Congress Catalog Card Number: 91-75802

ISBN: 0-15-543555-8

Copyright © 1992, 1988, 1984, 1979 by Harcourt Brace Jovanovich, Inc.

Address for Editorial Correspondence
Harcourt Brace Jovanovich College Publishers, 301 Commerce Street, Suite 3700, Fort Worth, TX 76102

Address for Orders
Harcourt Brace Jovanovich College Publishers, 6277 Sea Harbor Drive, Orlando, FL 32887
1-800-782-4479, or 1-800-433-0001 (in Florida)

Printed in the United States of America

    5 1 6 4 9 8 7 6 5 4

Harcourt Brace Jovanovich

Preface

Introductory Musicianship, now in its fourth edition, is a text-workbook in musical fundamentals that places particular emphasis on the basic skills of reading and writing music. It assumes students have no prior knowledge of music, and it is appropriate in either a one- or two-semester fundamentals course for nonmajors or in an introductory theory course for majors. The unusual organization of the book—five text units with worksheets, alternating with three units devoted entirely to rhythmic and melodic sight-reading exercises and rhythmic and melodic dictation exercises—allows a high degree of flexibility and has proved an invaluable feature of the book. This organization remains intact in this edition. In other respects, many changes have been made to strengthen and improve the book: the discussion of certain topics has been revised and reordered for greater clarity and simplicity; the worksheets have been reorganized to begin with the simplest exercise and conclude with the most difficult; sight-reading exercises have been expanded and revised; and Unit 8 has been extensively reorganized with a helpful new unit on melodic writing.

The text units present notation, meter, scales and modes, intervals, triads, seventh chords, and the basic principles of melodic writing, accompaniment, harmonization, transposition, and instrumental transposition. Like a foreign language, music must be experienced, not simply read about; therefore, the verbal explanations are brief and the music examples are copious.

Units 1, 3, 4, and 6 end with numerous worksheets, keyed in the margin to the corresponding text sections for the students' convenience in review. These worksheets, including an overall review test, recapitulate the entire contents of each unit and offer more than enough practice to give students ease and confidence in each particular skill. (The book has been laid out, incidentally, so that all textual material will remain intact for later reference after the students have torn out the worksheets and transferred them to their notebooks.)

Units 2, 5, and 7 present a large number of sight-reading exercises, carefully graded from easy to challengingly difficult. Each unit contains one-, two-, and three-part rhythmic exercises, melodic exercises, valuable coordinated melodic-rhythmic exercises, and rhythmic and melodic dictation examples, all of which include and reinforce the material in the text units. The students learn to count both divisions and subdivisions of the beat, and they learn three ways of singing the melodic exercises—by pitch name, by scale-degree number, and by either movable or fixed *do* solfeggio syllables. The sheer quantity of these exercises is one of their greatest virtues.

The addition of two-measure rhythmic and melodic dictation examples should be most helpful for student ear-training. Many of the early examples in Unit 2 are readily adaptable to classroom dictation. For the rhythmic exercises, the instructor can first name the note value to be used as the unit of beat, establish the meter and tempo by clapping two or three preliminary bars, and then clap the exercise, with the students writing the note values they hear and adding bar lines. This process should be repeated no more than three times for each exercise. Instructors can similarly adapt the melodic exercises. At first, the combination of rhythmic and melodic elements may pose too many problems. In such cases, the instructor can ignore meter signatures and note values, playing the melodies slowly, with an equal value for each note, and announcing both the first note and the clef. Later, when the students have gained ability and confidence in handling rhythm and melody separately, instructors can combine the two elements.

The organization of the book allows instructors to introduce subjects in whatever order they wish. Each unit is planned for a flexible approach. For example, the book presents two ways of constructing scales, two ways of inverting intervals, and two ways of transposing a melody. Furthermore, the book includes more material than instructors can probably cover in most one-semester courses—such as the introduction to twelve-tone technique in Unit 3, the information about commercial chords in Unit 6, and some of the most difficult exercises in Unit 7. Besides its obvious usefulness in the two-semester sequence, this material is included to motivate and challenge students to continue their exploration of these subjects on their own.

I extend my sincere thanks to my many friends for their support; to the Los Angeles Valley College music faculty and staff; to Dr. Woody James; to the many instructors across the country who have adopted previous editions and have shared their needs and recommendations; to Moonyeen Albrecht of Central Michigan University, Eddie del Rio of Miami-Dade Community College, Byron Gregory of Jackson State University, Jerry Laszloffy of University of Connecticut, Ruby Ronald of Washington State University, and Charles Warren of Arizona State University for their insightful reviews; and, most of all, to the students who have helped and inspired me in the development of this revised text. And I extend special thanks to the staff at Harcourt Brace Jovanovich—particularly Cindy Kumagawa, acquisitions editor; Diana Jean Parks, designer; Elizabeth Banks, art editor; Lynne Bush, production manager; Katherine Watson, production editor; and Cheryl Hauser, manuscript editor—for their encouragement, prodding, patience, hard work, and dedication to excellence.

Theodore A. Lynn

Contents

The Basics

1a The Staff

The **staff** (or stave) is a series of five lines and four spaces on which notes are written. A four-line staff is still in use for the notation of Gregorian chant (the chant of the Roman Catholic Church), but all other conventional notation always uses the five-line staff. Lines and spaces of the staff, for identification, are numbered from bottom to top.

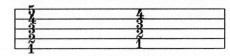

1b Clefs

A **clef** is a sign written at the beginning of the staff to indicate the pitch name—A, B, C, D, E, F, or G—for each line and space. There are three clef signs, representing the pitches G, F, and C, and the shape of the signs is a modification of the shape of these letters. The variety of clefs and clef positions results from the desire to avoid too many leger lines (see 1c1). Whenever the range of a voice or instrument exceeded the five-line staff, composers or music copyists would change the position of the clef or introduce another clef. In the following list of clefs, the arrow indicates the position of middle C (the C nearest the middle of the piano keyboard) as it is notated in each clef.

(1) G CLEF (TREBLE CLEF)

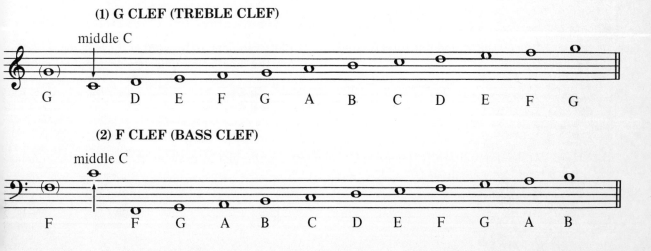

1

(3) C CLEF

Although in early music the G and F clefs were movable, they are now stationary. The C clef remains movable from one line to another, allowing the notes to remain within the staff. All five C clefs were commonly used until the middle of the eighteenth century, when composers gradually abandoned all but two of the positions, the alto and the tenor. The alto clef is still used to notate music for the viola, and the tenor clef is occasionally used for the cello, bassoon, and trombone.

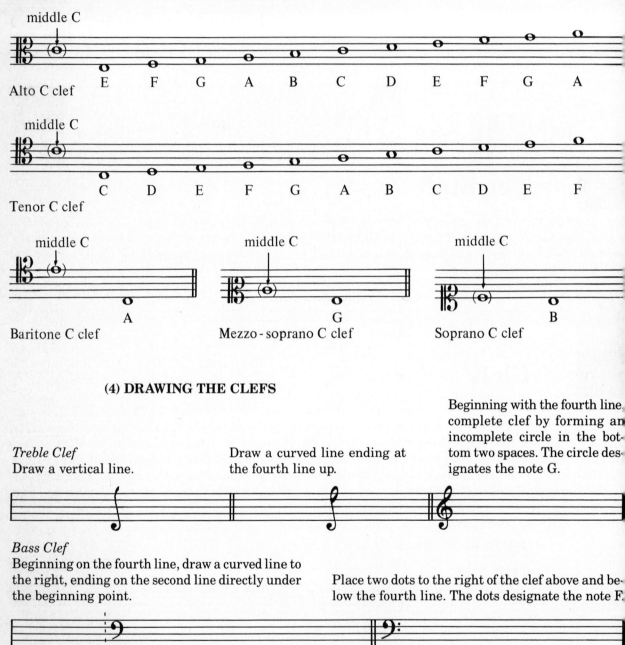

(4) DRAWING THE CLEFS

Treble Clef
Draw a vertical line.

Draw a curved line ending at the fourth line up.

Beginning with the fourth line, complete clef by forming an incomplete circle in the bottom two spaces. The circle designates the note G.

Bass Clef
Beginning on the fourth line, draw a curved line to the right, ending on the second line directly under the beginning point.

Place two dots to the right of the clef above and below the fourth line. The dots designate the note F.

C Clef
The original C clefs were literally the letter C. We now form this clef by drawing curved lines that enclose the line we wish to designate as C.

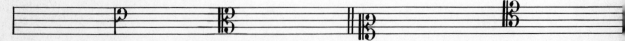

The **great staff** (or grand staff) is a double staff with both a treble clef and a bass clef. All the most frequently used pitches can be written on this staff. Middle C is placed between the two staves. The great staff can be considered an eleven-line staff with middle C occupying the short eleventh line, or leger line.

The piano keyboard is arranged in a pattern of seven white and five black keys and is repeated seven times on the modern 88-key piano. The black keys are in repeated patterns of two and then three. The note C is the first white key below the two black keys. Western music divides the pitch into half-steps (semitones): one key to the next *closest* key, white to black, black to white, and in the case of E-F and B-C, white to white. (See 1i.)

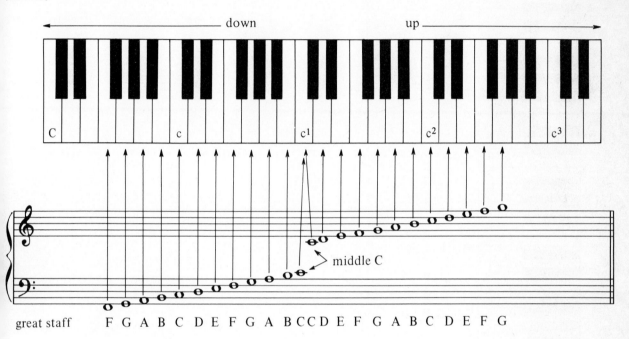

great staff   F G A B C D E F G A B C C D E F G A B C D E F G

(1) LEGER LINES

For notes beyond the range of the five-line staff, small line segments called **leger lines** (or ledger lines) are added above or below the staff, so that higher or lower notes may be written. Leger lines are spaced with the same distance between them as that between the lines of the staff. They are just wide enough to extend slightly to the left and right of the note.

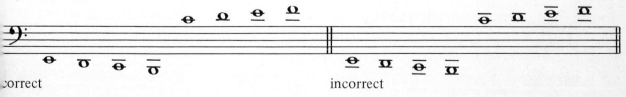

The note is placed on the last leger line or in the space beyond the last leger line. A leger line is *never* used beyond the note.

correct   incorrect

3

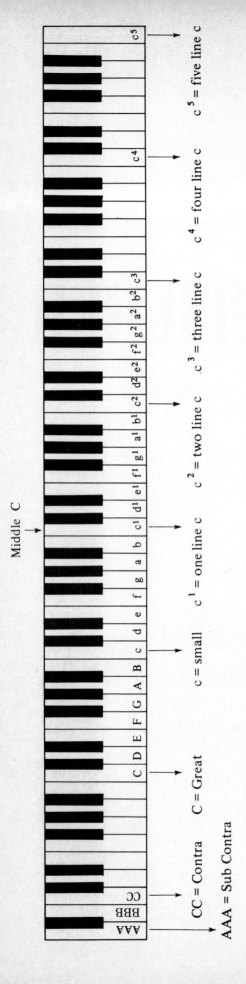

(2) KEYBOARD OCTAVE REGISTERS

The standard 88 piano keyboard has eight a, b, and c keys and seven d, e, f, and g keys. To enable you to describe clearly which "a" you are discussing, each octave register (c–b) has been assigned a specific letter register. Beginning with one octave below middle c of the piano, lowercase letters are used for the ascending octaves and uppercase letters for the descending octaves.

(3) OCTAVE SIGN *(8va)*

The range of the staff can be further extended with the **octave sign 8va**, indicating that the notes in the bracket are to be played an octave higher or lower. An octave is the pitch with the same name eight notes above or below the given pitch. The octave sign **15ma** indicates two octaves or fifteen pitches higher. The octave sign *8va* below a group of notes is not used in the treble and C clefs, and *15ma* below a group of notes is extremely rare.

F	G	F	G		G	F	G	F
written		sounded			written		sounded

 Notes

Notes are symbols indicating the relative duration, length, or pitch when placed on a staff. Beginning with the whole note, each succeeding note is divided by two.

double whole note (very rare)

1 whole note

equals

2 half notes

=

4 quarter notes

=

8 eighth notes

=

16 sixteenth notes

=

32 32nd notes   etc.

=

64 64th notes   etc.

(1) DOTTED NOTES

A dot after a note adds one half to the durational value of the note.

dotted whole note	𝅝·	equals	𝅝	plus 𝅗𝅥
dotted half note	𝅗𝅥·	=	𝅗𝅥	+ 𝅘𝅥
dotted quarter note	𝅘𝅥·	=	𝅘𝅥	+ 𝅘𝅥𝅮
dotted eighth note	𝅘𝅥𝅮·	=	𝅘𝅥𝅮	+ 𝅘𝅥𝅯
dotted sixteenth note	𝅘𝅥𝅯·	=	𝅘𝅥𝅯	+ 𝅘𝅥𝅰
dotted 32nd note	𝅘𝅥𝅰·	=	𝅘𝅥𝅰	+ 𝅘𝅥𝅱

A double dot may be added to a note. It adds one half plus one quarter to the value of the note.

double-dotted quarter note   𝅘𝅥·· = 𝅘𝅥 + 𝅘𝅥𝅮 + 𝅘𝅥𝅯

The dot is always added to the right side of the note. If the note is on a line, the dot is placed in the space above. If the note is in a space, the dot is placed in the same space.

(2) STEMS

As you just saw, all notes except whole notes have **stems**. Stems are drawn down if notes are above the middle line of the staff, and up if notes are below the middle line. Stems drawn up are placed on the right side of the note; stems drawn down are placed on the left side. For the middle-line note, stems may go up or down, but down is more usual.

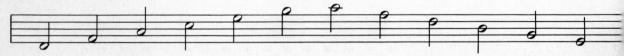

(3) FLAGS

Flags (or hooks) denote values shorter than a quarter note; they always extend to the right of the stem. Eighth notes have one flag, sixteenth notes have two flags, 32nd notes have three, and 64th notes have four.

(4) BEAMS

In instrumental music it is customary to use **beams**—horizontal lines—in place of flags for groups of eighth, sixteenth, 32nd, and 64th notes. The number of beams corresponds to the number of flags: one beam for eighth notes, two for sixteenth notes, and so on. Beams can be used with notes of different values, as long as they have values shorter than a quarter note. The combined note value of the beamed notes will generally equal a single beat as indicated by the meter signature (e.g., in ¼ the combined beamed notes will equal one quarter note).

In beaming several notes together, place the beam above if the majority of stems would normally go up. If the majority of stems would normally go down, the beams are placed below. Beams should more or less reflect, in a straight line, the overall contour of the note group.

(5) TIES AND SLURS

The *tie* is a curved line connecting two or more notes of the *same pitch*. The tie allows a note to be sustained across a bar line and is frequently used to arrive at a note value that is not available—a quarter note tied to a dotted quarter note, for example, produces a five-eighth note. The tied notes are not articulated but are sustained as a single note reflecting the value of the tied notes.

A tie is necessary if a note is held beyond a bar line or if the same note is connected across two or more measures.

A curved line placed above or below a group of *different* notes is called a **slur**. It indicates that the notes are to be performed *legato*, smoothly connected with no breaks between them.

1e Rests

Rests indicate silence. Each note value has its corresponding rest sign. Rests are never tied, since a succession of rests produces an uninterrupted silence without any additional sign.

𝗈	whole rest	▬	dotted whole rest	▬· or ▬ ▬
𝅗𝅥	half rest	▬	dotted half rest	▬· or 𝄼
♩	quarter rest	𝄽	dotted quarter rest	𝄽· or 𝄽 𝄾
♪	eighth rest	𝄾	dotted eighth rest	𝄾· or 𝄾 𝄿
𝅘𝅥𝅯	sixteenth rest	𝄿	dotted sixteenth rest	𝄿· or 𝄿 𝅀
𝅘𝅥𝅰	32nd rest	𝅀	dotted 32nd rest	𝅀· or 𝅀 𝅁
𝅘𝅥𝅱	64th rest	𝅁	dotted 64th rest	𝅁· or 𝅁 𝅂

A whole rest serves as a full measure rest in any and all meters. Double-dotted rests are possible. As with notes, the double dot adds one half plus one quarter value to the rest.

In ensemble music, parts may have several measures of rest at a time. A long rest sign, with a number above, indicates the number of measures of rest. The rest sign is drawn through the center line.

8 - measure rest

Meter Signatures

The **meter signature** (or time signature) at the beginning of a piece indicates a recurring pattern of accented and unaccented *beats* (or *pulses*) that generally remains unaltered throughout. The top number of the meter signature indicates the number of beats in the pattern, and the bottom number indicates the note (or rest) value of the beat. The recurring patterns are grouped into *bars*, or *measures*, and are separated from each other on the staff by a *bar line*. The first beat in each bar receives the main accent or stress ('). Sometimes another beat or other beats in the bar receive a secondary stress (–). The remaining beats are unstressed (∪).

2 →two beats in the bar
4 →quarter note gets one beat

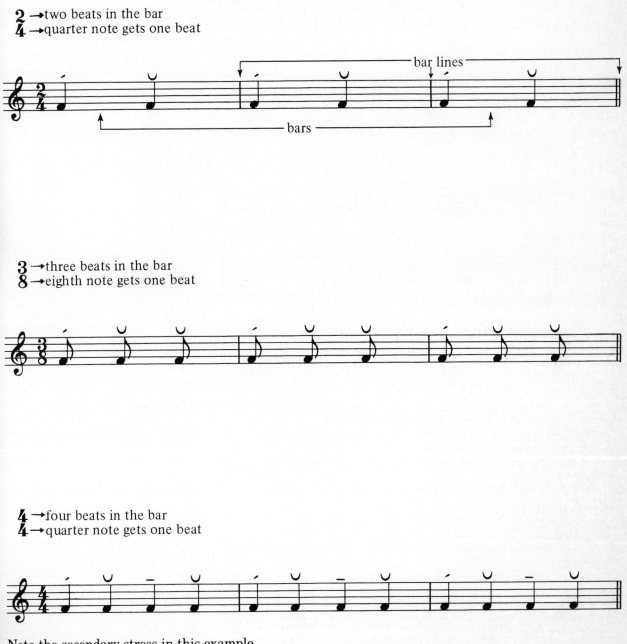

3 →three beats in the bar
8 →eighth note gets one beat

4 →four beats in the bar
4 →quarter note gets one beat

Note the secondary stress in this example.

Meter signatures generally fall into two categories. Basically, simple meters divide the beat into two; compound meters divide the beat into three. Further subdivision for both meter types subdivide into multiples of two.

Following is a list of the most common simple and compound meters, with stressed and unstressed beats indicated.

(1) SIMPLE METERS

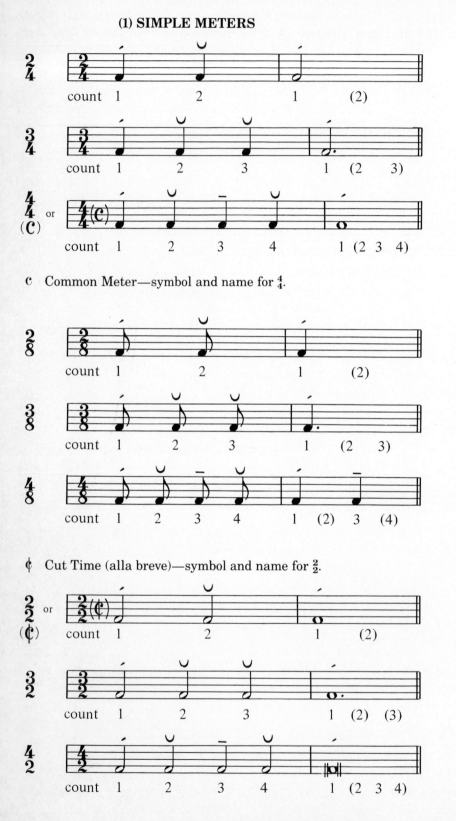

c Common Meter—symbol and name for $\frac{4}{4}$.

¢ Cut Time (alla breve)—symbol and name for $\frac{2}{2}$.

(2) COMPOUND METERS

Compound meters, such as $\frac{6}{8}$, $\frac{9}{8}$, and $\frac{12}{8}$, differ from the preceding simple meters in that the beat falls in groups of *three*.

two groups of three

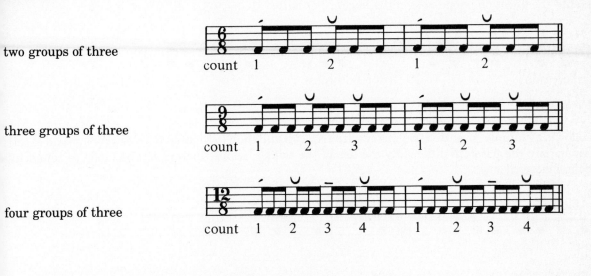

three groups of three

four groups of three

In compound meters played at a slow tempo, or speed, the eighth note receives one beat, the quarter note receives two beats, and the dotted quarter note receives three beats.

In a fast tempo, which is more usual for compound meters, the dotted quarter note receives one beat, the dotted half note receives two beats, and the tied dotted half and dotted quarter receives three beats.

But the most important thing to remember about compound meters is how they differ from simple meters. It is easy to distinguish the two types by remembering that simple meters divide the beat into groups of *two*, while compound meters divide the beat into groups of *three*.

(3) UNEQUAL METRICAL DIVISIONS

In twentieth-century music, meter signatures with **unequal divisions** of the measure, such as $\frac{5}{4}$, $\frac{5}{8}$, $\frac{7}{4}$, and $\frac{7}{8}$, are widely used. $\frac{5}{8}$ and $\frac{7}{8}$ can be clearly defined by the use of beams.

The possibilities for other unequal divisions are limited only by the composer's imagination.

(4) TRIPLETS AND DUPLETS

A *triplet* is a "borrowed" grouping of three in an otherwise normal pattern of division by two. Triplets are indicated by a slur or bracket and a *3* over the notes. Any note value may be used to form triplets, although the eighth-note triplet is the most often used. What all triplets have in common is that their total duration is equal to the duration of one note of the *next larger value*.

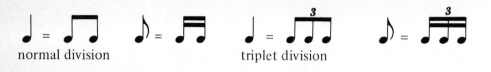

normal division   triplet division

The following example is written in $\frac{2}{4}$ meter with triplets, and then in $\frac{6}{8}$ meter. Both versions sound exactly the same; only the notation differs. By the use of the triplet, simple meters can be made to sound like compound meters.

simple

compound

A *duplet* is a "borrowed" grouping of two in an otherwise normal pattern of division by three (compound meters). Duplets are indicated by a slur or bracket and a *2* over the notes. Any note value may be used to form duplets, although the eight-note duplet is most often used.

normal division   duplet division

The following example is written first in $\frac{6}{8}$ meter with duplets and then in $\frac{2}{4}$ meter. Both versions sound exactly the same; only the notation differs. By use of the duplet, compound meters can be made to sound like simple meters.

Compound

Simple

Double Bars

A **double bar** is placed at the end of a work. It consists of a narrow bar line and a wider bar line.

A double bar with two narrow bar lines designates the end of part of a work or section, but not the final close.

The Anacrusis

A composition does not always begin on the first beat of the first measure. One or several notes can occur beforehand. This note is called an **anacrusis** (or upbeat or pick-up note). In vocal music, an anacrusis occurs when one or more unstressed syllables appears before the first stressed syllable.

The / cow jumped / over the / moon.

Customarily, the number of beats or the fraction of a beat used in the anacrusis is subtracted from the last measure of the work.

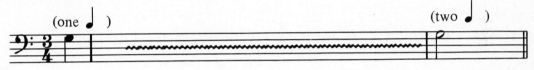

Half Steps and Whole Steps

In most Western music, the smallest interval, or distance, between two tones is a **half step** (semitone).

Two consecutive half steps combined make a **whole step**. Looking at the piano keyboard, you will notice a black key between C and D. The distance from C up to that black key is a half step. From the black key to D is a second half step. The two half steps combined result in a whole step. The nearest key, black or white, above or below any other key is a half step. Therefore, the next white key above B or E, or below C or F, is a half step.

Half steps may be either *chromatic* or *diatonic*. Chromatic half steps employ the same letter name (e.g., F to F♯ or B to B♭). Diatonic half steps employ adjacent letter names (e.g., F to G♭ or B to A♯).

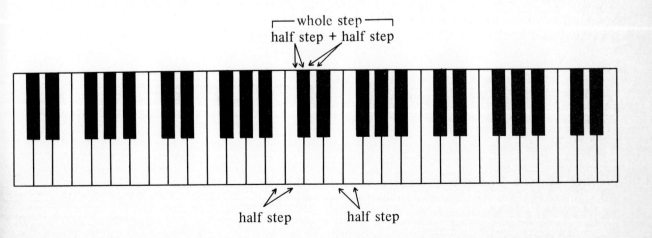

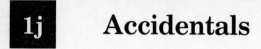

1j Accidentals

Accidentals are sharps, flats, or naturals introduced within the body of a work—in contrast to the sharps or flats found in the key signature. An accidental is always placed in front of the note it affects.

A **sharp** (♯) raises the pitch of a tone by a half step.
A **flat** (♭) lowers the pitch of a tone by a half step.

A **natural** (♮) is used to cancel a sharp or flat within a measure.

Except for the accidentals in the key signature (3c), the bar line cancels all accidentals in a previous measure.

Except for the accidentals in the key signature, an accidental affects a note only in the measure in which it appears, and only on that one line or space. For example, the second note in this measure is F♮.

A **double flat** (♭♭) lowers the pitch of a tone by two half steps.
A **double sharp** (×) raises the pitch of a tone by two half steps.

To cancel a double sharp or flat within the measure, only a single natural sign is required.

To cancel part of a double sharp or flat, a natural sign and the sharp or flat sign may be used but is not necessary. A single sharp or flat is sufficient.

1k Enharmonic Equivalents

With the exception of G# and A♭, every tone can have three different names, as shown below. Tones that are named differently but that sound the same are called **enharmonic equivalents**.

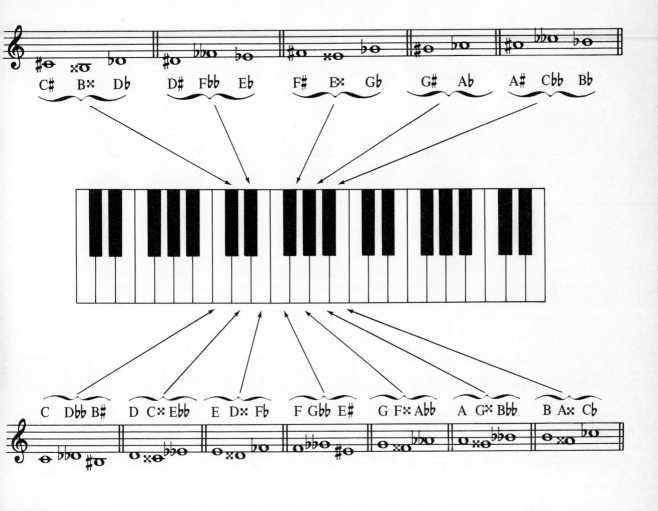

1l Repeat Signs

(1) D.C., D.S., CODA, AND FINE

Several kinds of **repeat signs** are used to direct the performer to skip back or forward through a work. These signs are used to avoid writing out long repeated passages.

D.C. (*da capo*)—repeat from the beginning
D.S. (*dal segno*)—repeat from the sign (𝄋)
fine—the end
D.C. al fine (*da capo al fine*)—repeat from the beginning to the end (the word *fine*)
D.S. al fine (*dal segno al fine*)—repeat from the sign (𝄋) to the end (the word *fine*)
coda—a section at the end of a work
D.C. al coda—repeat from the beginning to the coda sign (⊕) and then skip to the coda
D.S. al coda—repeat from the sign (𝄋) to the coda sign (⊕) and then skip to the coda

Sometimes the double bar with two dots is used in pairs to indicate a repeat. The measure(s) within the repeat signs are played twice. The repeat signs always have two dots on the inside, facing the measure(s) to be repeated. If the repeat is to the beginning of a work, a sign at the beginning is not required.

repeat signs

is played

(2) FIRST AND SECOND ENDINGS

Sometimes, when music repeats, first and second endings are used in order to save space. The first ending, which has a repeat sign, is played only the first time through. The second time through, the first ending is skipped over and the second ending is played.

is played

Another repeat sign, frequently seen in contemporary commercial music, is a sign indicating the repeating of one or two measures. In patterns that are repeated over and over, this method proves a time-saver for both the composer and the copyist. A one-measure repeat is represented by the sign placed inside one measure.

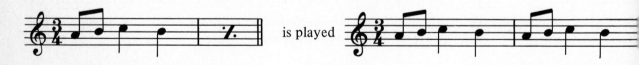

is played

A two-measure repeat is represented by the sign bridging two measures, with a 2 placed above the staff.

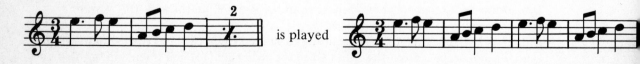

is played

16

Worksheet 1-1   NAME _____

Write the name of each of the following notes below the note.

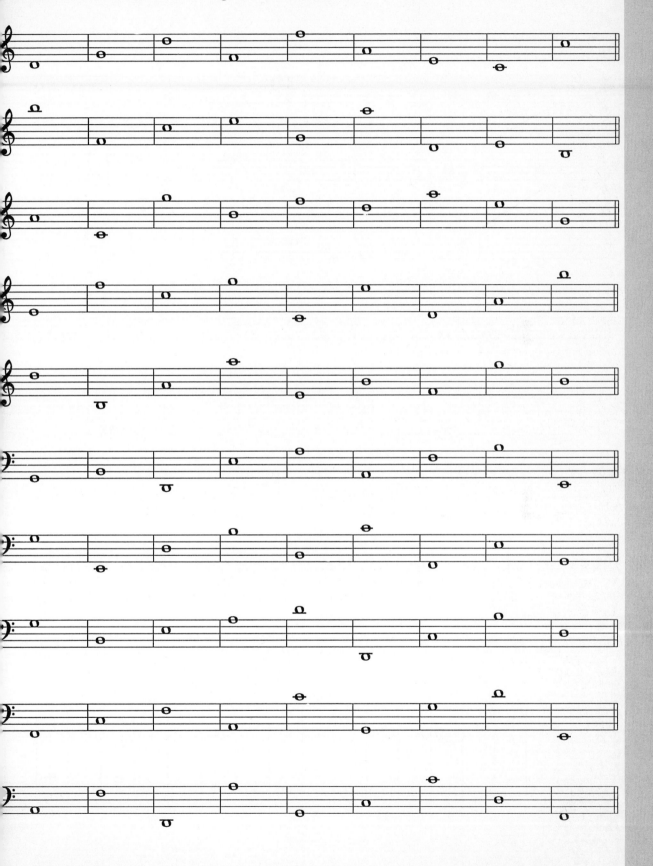

Worksheet 1-2

ıb Write the name of each of the following notes below the note.

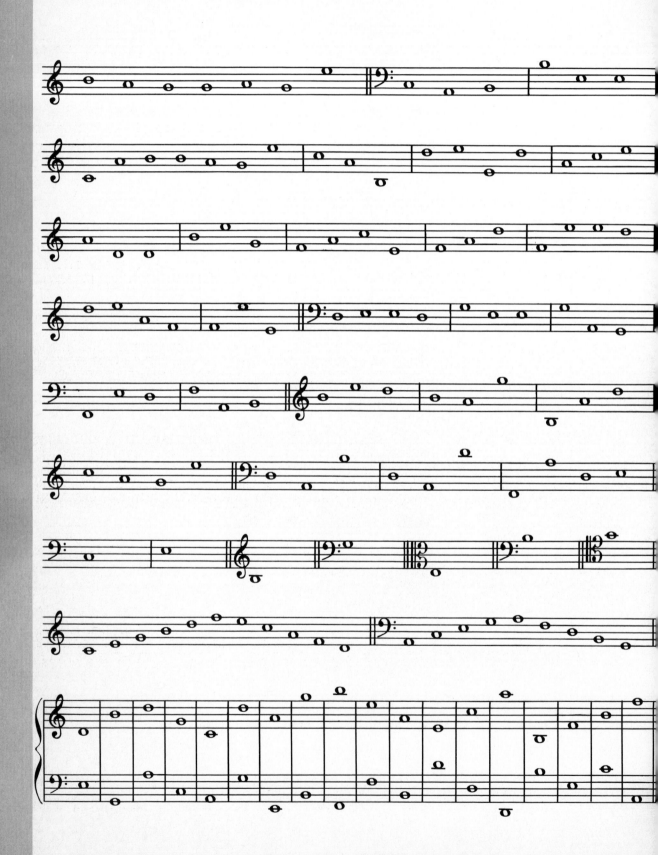

Worksheet 1-3

Write and name notes one octave *below* the given notes.

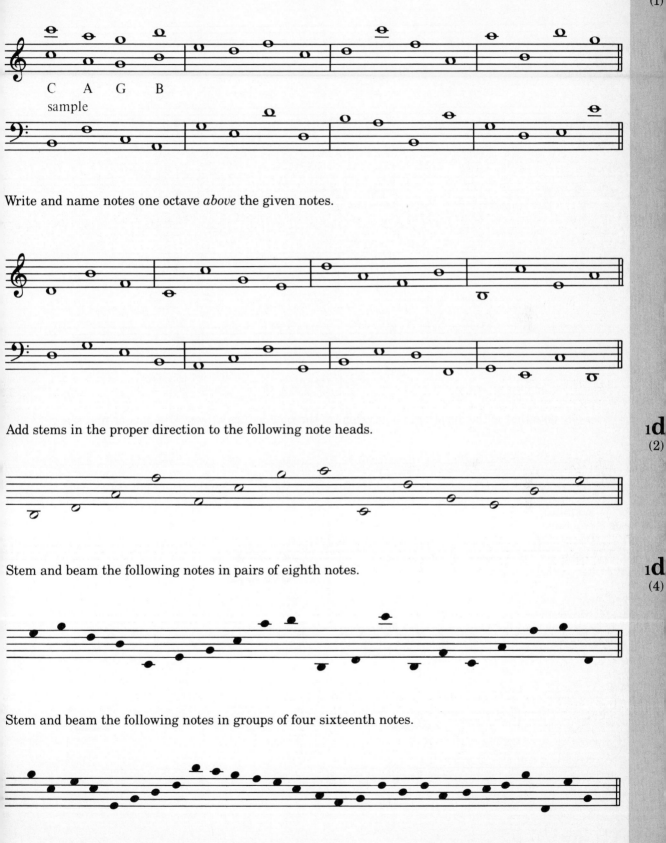

C   A   G   B
sample

Write and name notes one octave *above* the given notes.

Add stems in the proper direction to the following note heads.

Stem and beam the following notes in pairs of eighth notes.

Stem and beam the following notes in groups of four sixteenth notes.

1d Divide the following notes into the correct number of smaller notes indicated in parentheses.

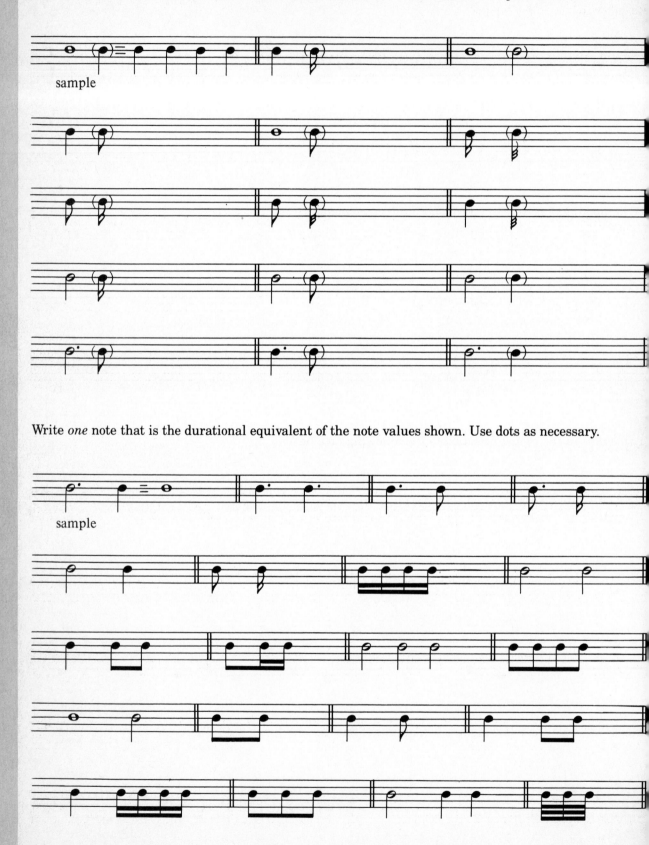

sample

Write *one* note that is the durational equivalent of the note values shown. Use dots as necessary.

sample

Give a simplified notation for the rhythms below, substituting *one note*, with a dot if necessary, for each set of tied notes, as in the sample.

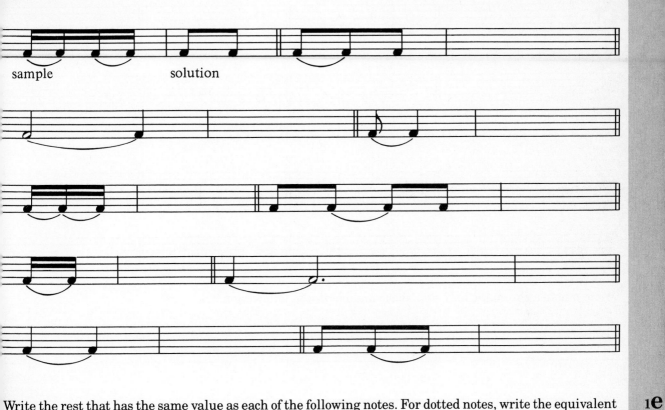

sample   solution

Write the rest that has the same value as each of the following notes. For dotted notes, write the equivalent rests *without using dots*.   **1e**

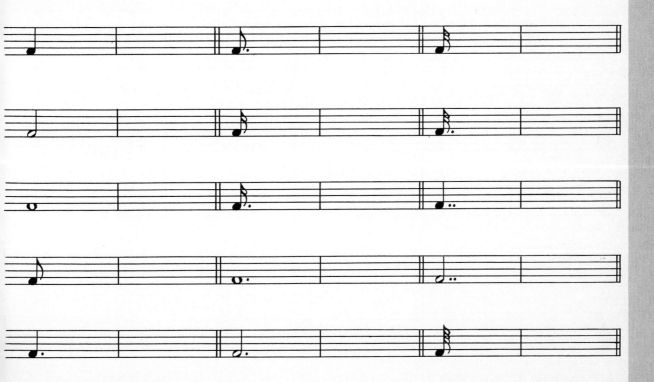

1i

Write a note a diatonic whole step above and below the following notes.

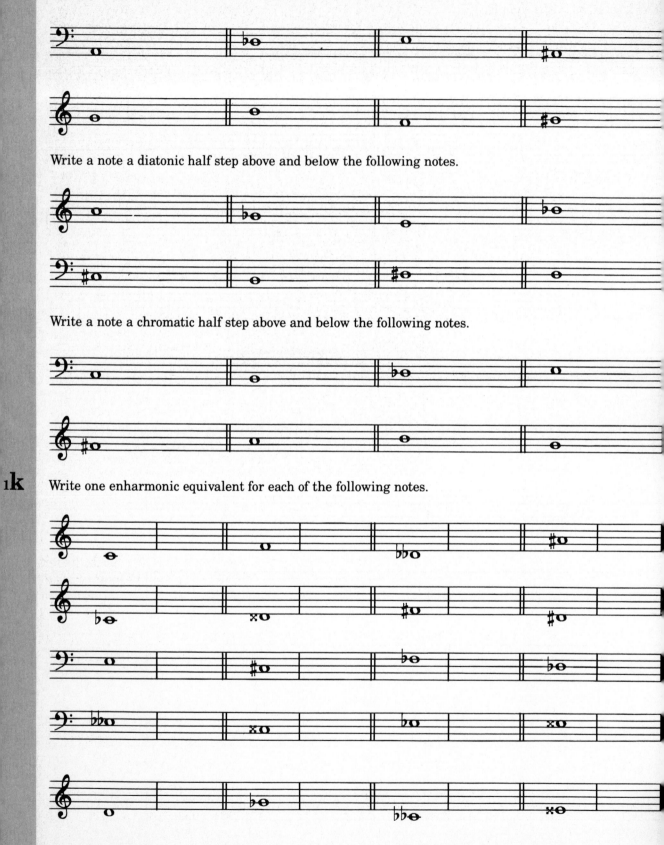

Write a note a diatonic half step above and below the following notes.

Write a note a chromatic half step above and below the following notes.

1k

Write one enharmonic equivalent for each of the following notes.

Worksheet 1-7

Place correct bar lines in each of the following rhythmic exercises.

if

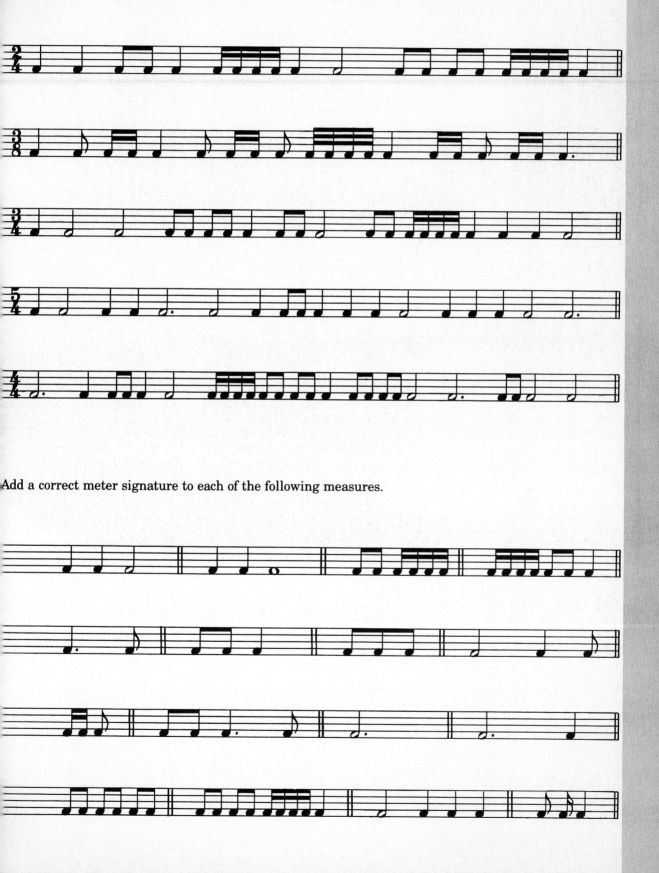

Add a correct meter signature to each of the following measures.

Worksheet 1-8

Each of the following measures is rhythmically incomplete. Complete each measure by adding *one note o*
the proper value, as in the sample.

sample

solution

Place correct bar lines in each of the following rhythmic exercises.

Add a correct meter signature to each of the following measures. Be sure you understand the distinction between simple and compound meters (1f2).

Review of Unit 1

1b 1. Write the name of each of the following notes below the note.

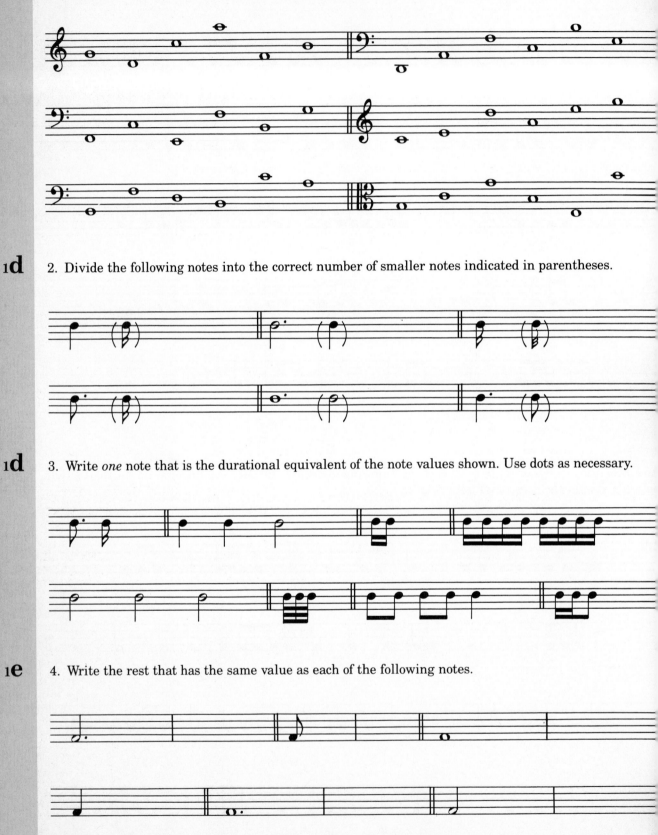

1d 2. Divide the following notes into the correct number of smaller notes indicated in parentheses.

1d 3. Write *one* note that is the durational equivalent of the note values shown. Use dots as necessary.

1e 4. Write the rest that has the same value as each of the following notes.

5. Write a note a diatonic whole step above and below the following notes.

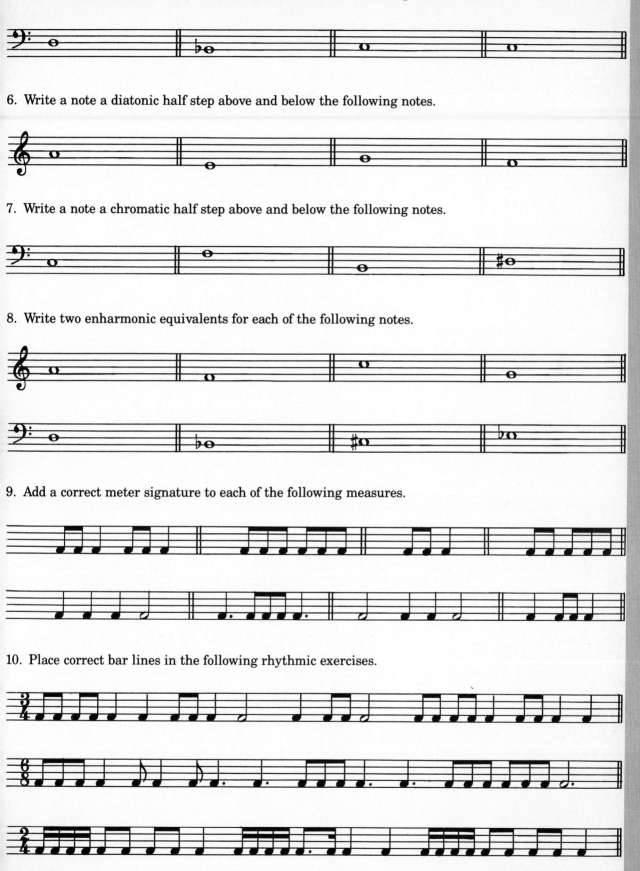

6. Write a note a diatonic half step above and below the following notes.

7. Write a note a chromatic half step above and below the following notes.

8. Write two enharmonic equivalents for each of the following notes.

9. Add a correct meter signature to each of the following measures.

10. Place correct bar lines in the following rhythmic exercises.

2

Rhythmic and Melodic Exercises—Easy

Rhythmic Exercises: Group 1

The following suggestions will help you establish good practice habits in these rhythmic exercises.

1. Before beginning, establish a moderate tempo, tapping your foot for at least two measures. On the metronome, a setting of 80 or 84 (that is, 80 or 84 beats per minute) will be comfortable. If you do not have a metronome, use a watch with a second hand and tap a bit faster than once per second. *Never practice too fast*; it is the downfall of all beginners.
2. Clap the strong beats louder than the weaker beats. For notes with more than one beat, clap the first beat aloud and silently clap the remaining beats. In $\frac{4}{4}$ for example, the whole note will be clapped aloud on one and silently clapped on two, three, and four.
3. *Count out loud.* For notes that last more than one beat, count the first beat aloud and whisper the remaining beats. In the first few exercises, the beats that are to be silently clapped and whispered appear in parentheses. In later exercises, write the beat numbers below the notes only if absolutely necessary.

(1) SIMPLE METERS WITH NO BEAT DIVISION, USING o, ♩, ♩., AND ♩

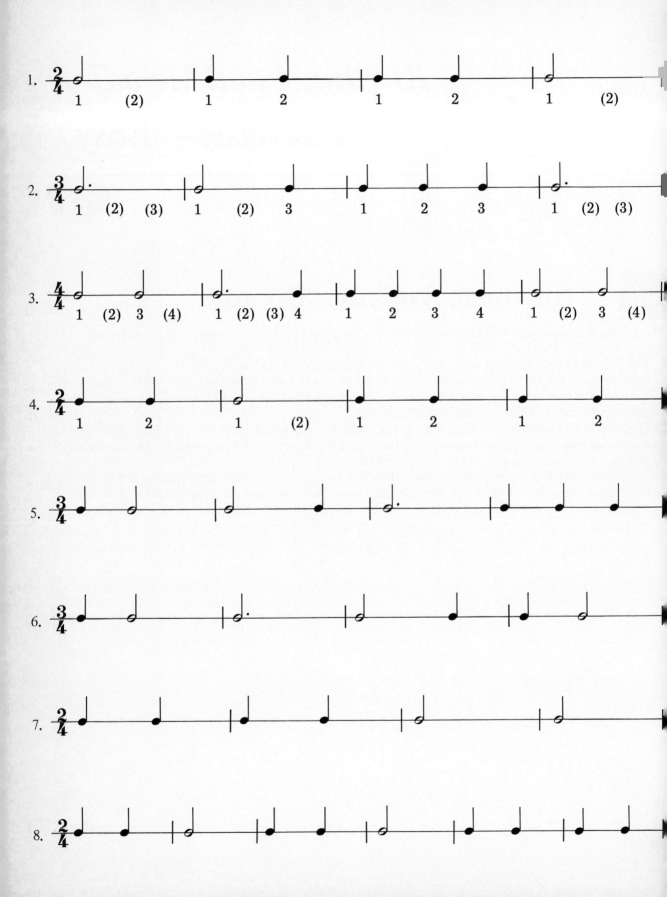

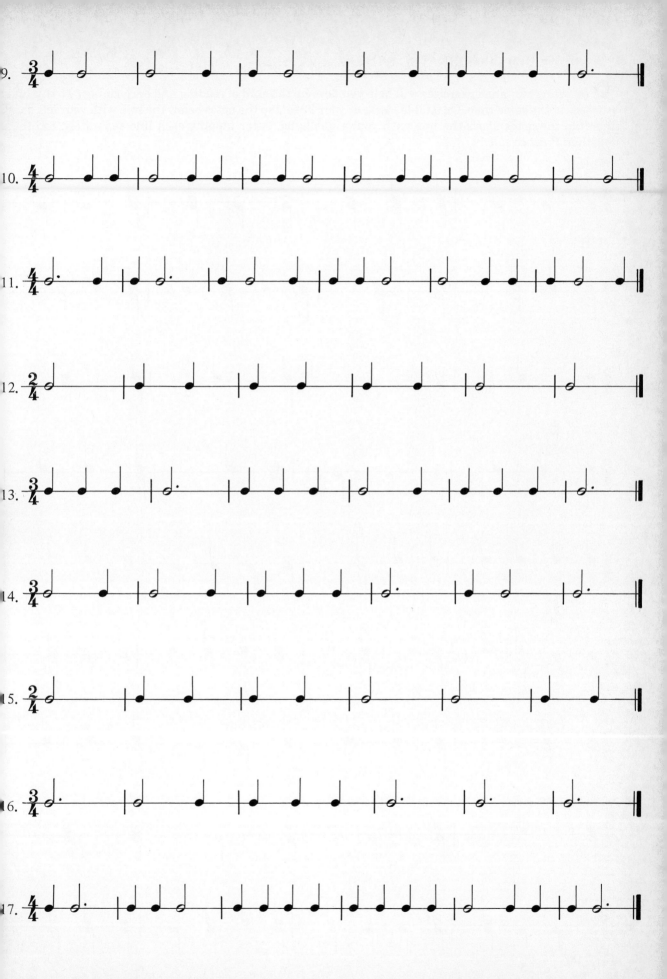

(2) COORDINATED-SKILL EXERCISES

The following two-hand exercises will help you develop the skill of reading and performing two rhythmic patterns at the same time. On a table, desk, or your knee, tap the notes below the line with your left hand, then tap the notes above the line with your right hand. After tapping each line separately, tap them together. *Practice slowly.*

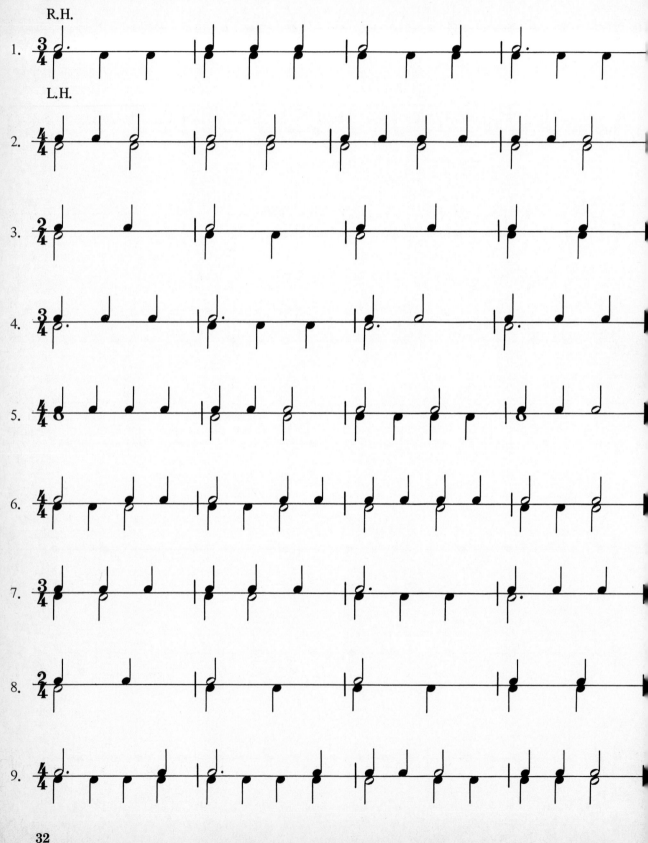

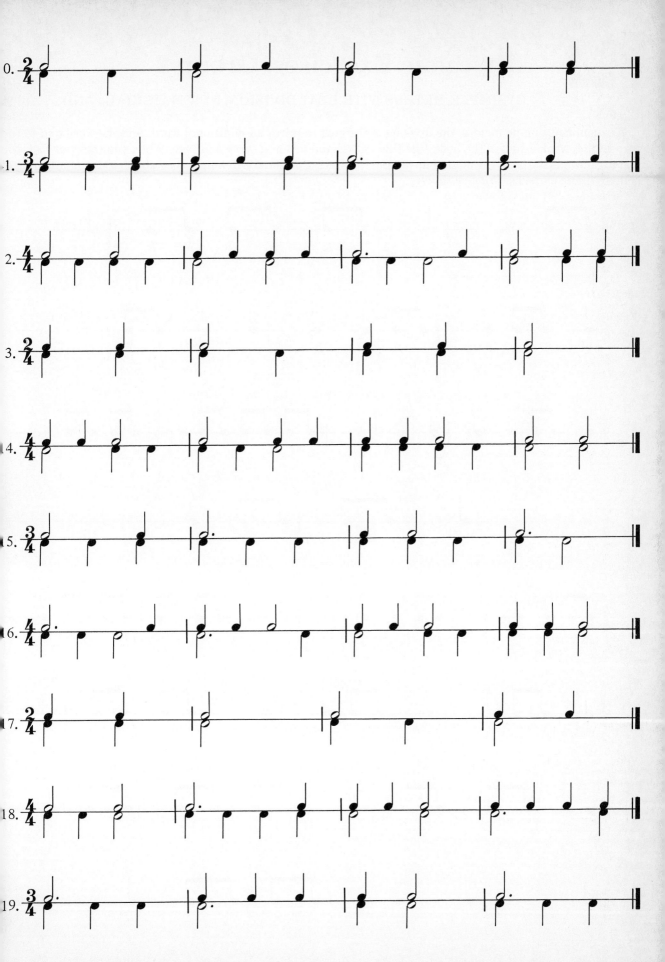

2b Rhythmic Exercises: Group 2

(1) SIMPLE METERS WITH BEAT DIVISION; NEW MATERIAL ♪ AND ♫

In counting simple meters, the division of the beat requires an additional word. Add the word *and* to the second, weaker half of the beat, like this: "ONE-and *two*-and *three*-and," etc. When you tap your foot, the tap down is the beat, the motion up is "and." Counting out loud will help you establish a stronger feeling of rhythmic patterns. *Practice slowly.*

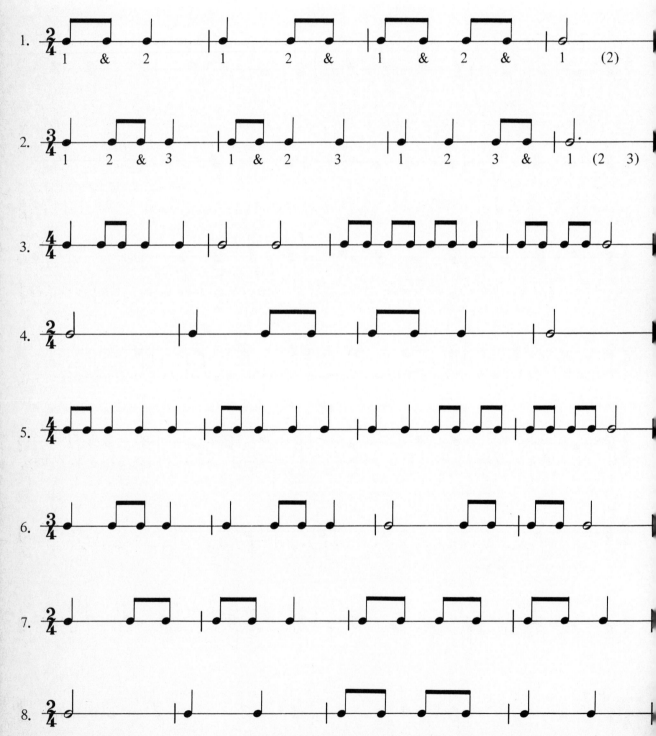

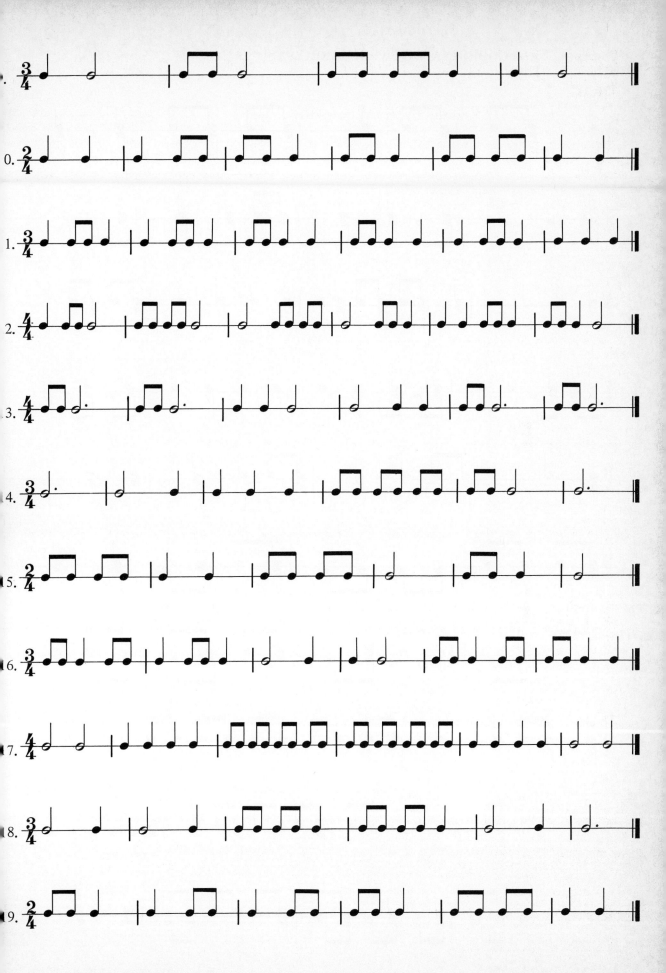

(2) COORDINATED-SKILL EXERCISES

37

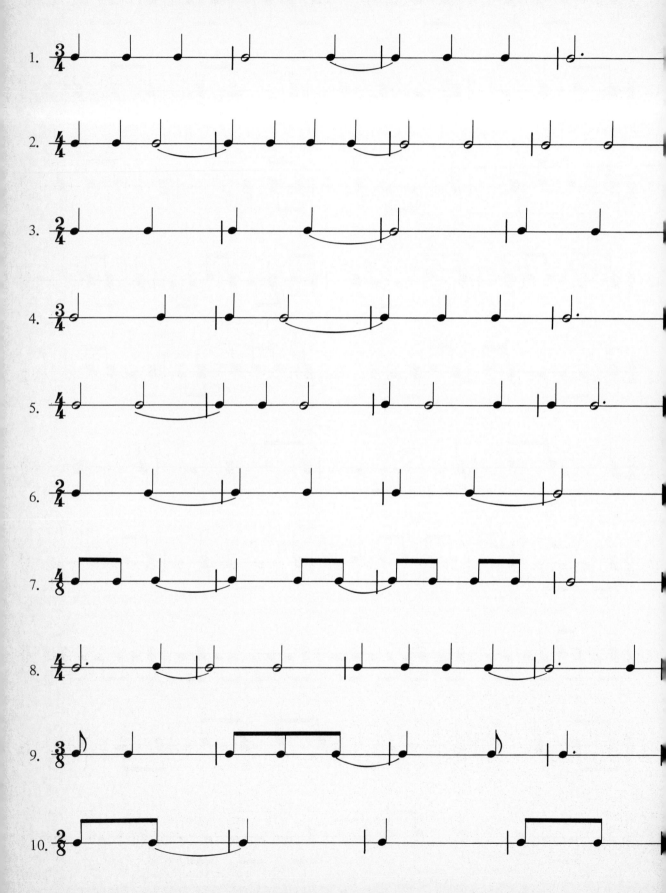

39

(4) EIGHT-MEASURE EXERCISES

41

(5) COORDINATED-SKILL EXERCISES

(1) SIMPLE METERS WITH BEAT SUBDIVISION; NEW MATERIAL ♪, ♫ AND ♩♪

In simple meters, the subdivision of the beat requires additional words. In the division of the beat, we added the word *and*. We now add the syllable *eh* between the beat and the word *and*, then the syllable *ah* after the *and*. In the subdivision of the quarter note, the word *and* remains on the second half of the beat. For an accurate performance of the dotted quarter and eighth (♩♪), count the division of the beat tapping the note on the appropriate word. ♩.   ♪

1 (& 2) & in simple meters $\frac{2}{4}$, $\frac{3}{4}$, $\frac{4}{4}$

(2) EIGHT-MEASURE EXERCISES

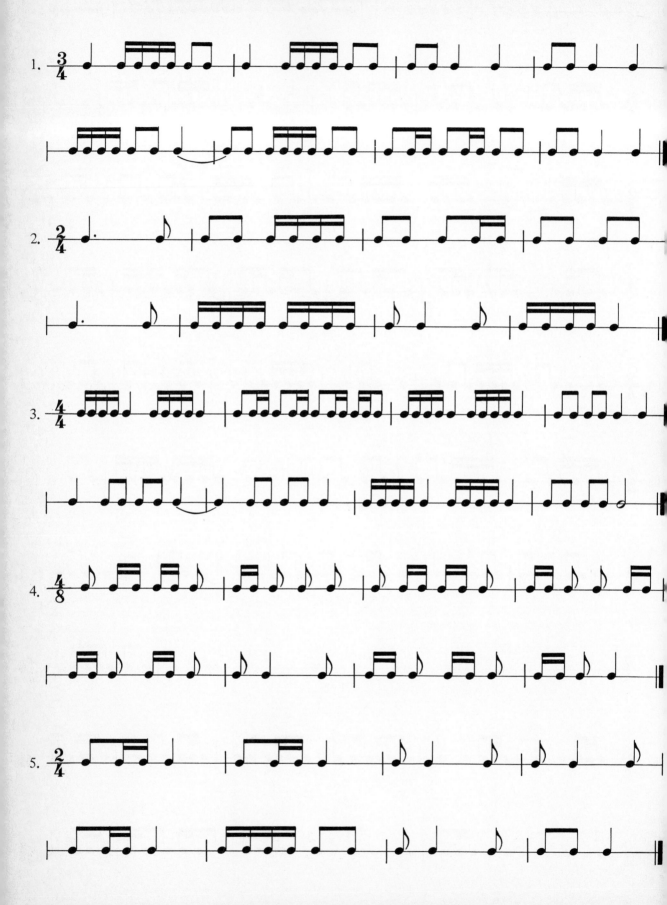

(5) EIGHT-MEASURE EXERCISES

(6) COORDINATED-SKILL EXERCISES

(7) THREE-PART RHYTHMIC EXERCISES

These exercises are for group participation, with at least one person on each line. Divide the parts among the performers, establish a beat, and begin. Perform each exercise a second and third time, with the performers tapping a different part each time.

You can use these exercises on your own to further develop your skill of reading multiple musical lines. Practice lines 1 and 2, then lines 2 and 3, and then lines 1 and 3.

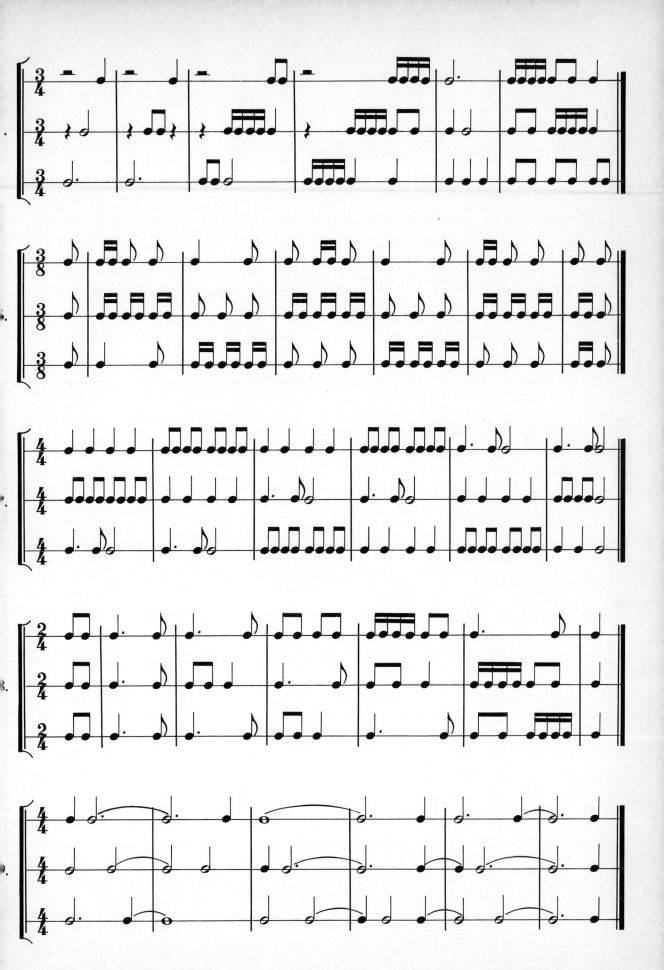

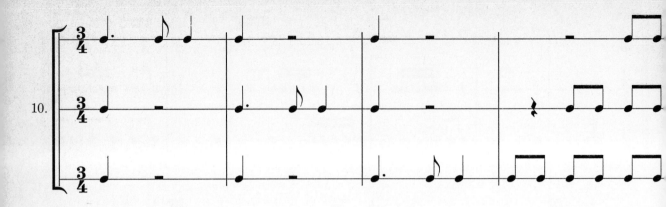

10.

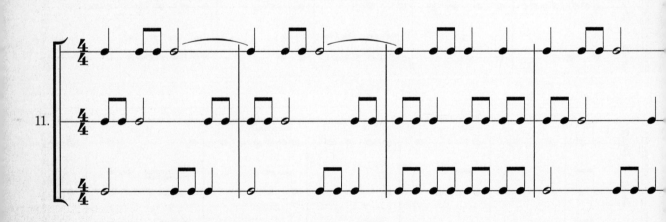

11.

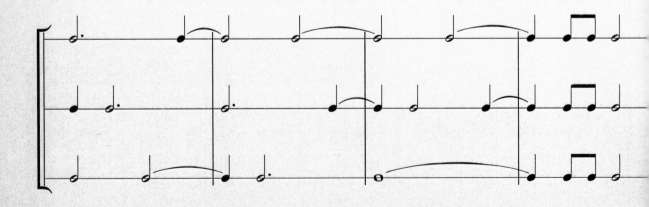

Melodic Exercises: Group 1

The following suggestions will help you develop good practice habits in these singing exercises.

1. Each singing example should first be clapped as a rhythmic exercise.
2. It should then be sung, using the letter names of the notes (and singing it an octave higher or lower if it is uncomfortable for your range as written).
3. It should then be sung again, using the *number system*, in which the numbers 1-2-3-4-5-6-7 are assigned to the notes of the scale in any key (3a). For example: in the key of C, C is 1, D is 2, E is 3, etc; in the key of F, F is 1, G is 2, A is 3, etc.

(1) SIMPLE METERS WITH NO BEAT DIVISION

(2) COORDINATED MELODIC-RHYTHMIC EXERCISES

Similar to the coordinated rhythmic exercises, these exercises combine two musical activities—this time, singing and clapping. Learn each line separately, then combine the two skills. If possible, sing the melodic line with pitch names or numbers, but if you find the combination of singing and clapping too difficult, sing the melodic line on a neutral syllable. *Practice slowly.*

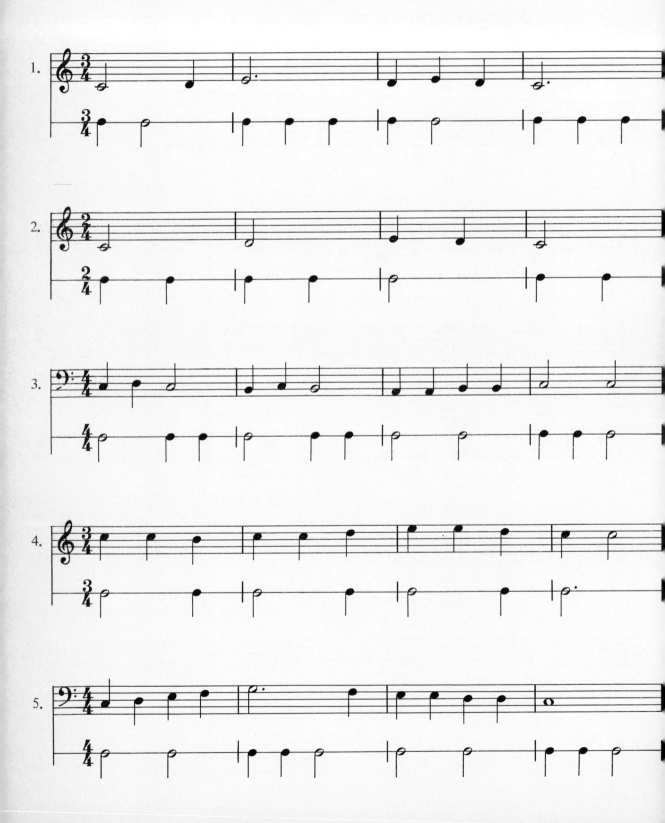

63

For longer rhythmic dictation examples combine any two or three exercises, of similar meter signatures into a single exercise.

RHYTHMIC DICTATION

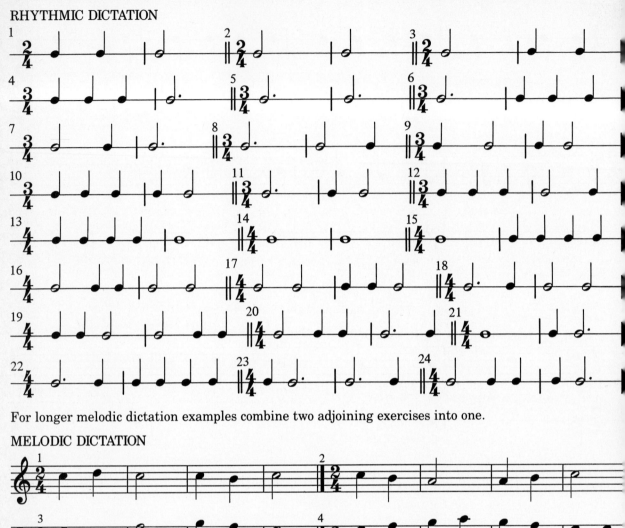

For longer melodic dictation examples combine two adjoining exercises into one.

MELODIC DICTATION

Melodic Exercises: Group 2

(1) SIMPLE METERS WITH BEAT DIVISION

Periodically, chord names and roman numerals will appear above and below a given melody. These allow a musician to add the correct chord (Unit 6) accompaniment to a given melody. The letters placed above the music, a common practice in commercial music, indicate the chord to be used for that measure or beat. Uppercase letters are Major triads (6a1). The roman numbers placed below the music, more common in the academic study of music, indicate a chord based on the diatonic scale.

The following melody is in F Major. The F Major scale is numbered one through seven, one being F, two, G, three, A, and so forth. In this example, I is an F chord, IV is a B♭ chord, and V is a C chord.

(2) COORDINATED MELODIC-RHYTHMIC EXERCISES

6.

7.

8.

9.

10.

For longer rhythmic dictation examples combine any two or three exercises, of similar meter signatures, into a single exercise.

RHYTHMIC DICTATION

For longer melodic dictation examples combine two adjoining exercises into one.

MELODIC DICTATION

(3) EIGHT-MEASURE EXERCISES

6.

7.

8.

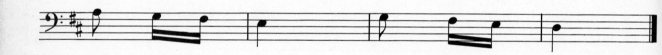

9.

10.

(4) COORDINATED MELODIC-RHYTHMIC EXERCISES

For longer rhythmic dictation examples combine any two or three exercises, of similar meter signatures, into a single exercise.

RHYTHMIC DICTATION

For longer melodic dictation examples combine two adjoining exercises into one.

MELODIC DICTATION

Melodic Exercises: Group 3

(1) SIMPLE METERS WITH BEAT DIVISION AND SUBDIVISION

6.

7.

8.

9.

10.

Round Form

A round requires the performers to be divided into three or four equal groups. Each group will perform the complete work. The first group begins at the opening phrase (1), the second, starting at the beginning, enters when the first group reaches the second phrase (2), and so on. Rounds may be repeated as many times as you wish.

(2) COORDINATED MELODIC-RHYTHMIC EXERCISES

1.
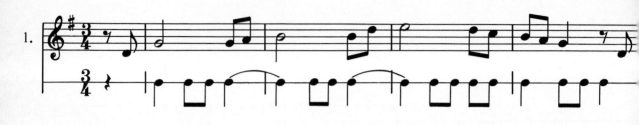

2.

3.

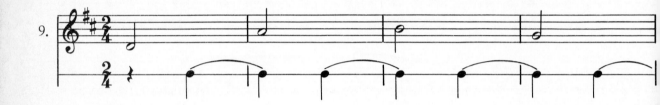

For longer rhythmic dictation examples combine any two or three exercises, of similar meter signatures, into a single exercise.

RHYTHMIC DICTATION

For longer melodic dictation examples combine two adjoining exercises into one.

MELODIC DICTATION

3

Scales, Keys, and Modes

3a   Scales

A **scale** (from Italian *scala*, ladder) is an ordered series of pitches, going either up or down. There are many forms of scales, but the two most commonly used in Western music since the seventeenth century are the forms called *major* and *minor*. The major scale is represented by the white keys of the piano that span the octave C to C. The ascending major-scale arrangement of whole steps and half steps is as follows: a whole step between the first and second and the second and third pitches, a half step between the third and fourth, a whole step between the fourth and fifth, the fifth and sixth, and the sixth and seventh pitches, then a half step between the seventh and eighth pitches. The following major scale is represented C to C.

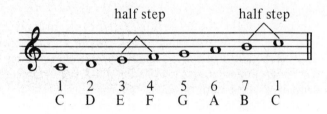

half step   half step

1	2	3	4	5	6	7	1
C	D	E	F	G	A	B	C

3b   Circle of Fifths—Major Keys

A scale that follows the half-step and whole-step pattern described is called a Major *diatonic* (or natural) scale. With this half-step and whole-step pattern kept consistent, the major scale can be transposed (moved) to all the remaining eleven half steps within the octave. For each transposition, sharps or flats must be added to maintain the correct diatonic pattern.

The major scales and their appropriate sharps or flats can be arranged in a sequence called the **circle of fifths**, shown in the diagram on page 86. With C at the top, the fifths lead clockwise to G, then to D, and so on around the circle back to C. Note that the scales requiring sharps are clockwise *ascending* fifths, and that the scales requiring flats are counterclockwise *descending* fifths. Note also that at the bottom of the circle, the scales with sharps and flats must cross. These three sets of scales, each with two key signatures, are called *enharmonic* major scales. (See 1k.)

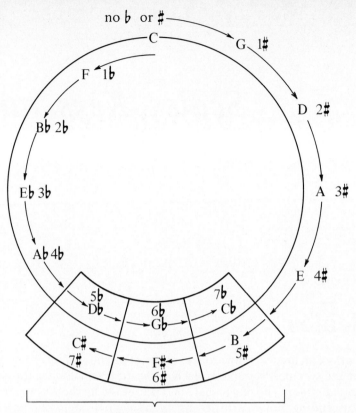

no ♭ or ♯ ——
C
G 1♯
F 1♭
D 2♯
B♭ 2♭
E♭ 3♭
A 3♯
A♭ 4♭
E 4♯
5♭
D♭
6♭
G♭
7♭
C♭
C♯
7♯
F♯
6♯
B
5♯

enharmonic keys

3c Key Signatures

In music based on a major or minor scale, the piece often centers on a specific tone, the first note of the scale. This tone is called the *tonic* (or keynote or key center). Playing a G major scale or a piece using this scale means playing in the *key* of G major. The sharps or flats used in a particular key are grouped together at the beginning of the staff in an arrangement called the *key signature*. Any sharp or flat shown in the key signature means that the corresponding note is played sharped or flatted throughout a composition— although the sharp or flat may be canceled with a natural sign (♮) for a single measure (see 1j).

The sequence of sharps or flats in a *key signature* follows a specific order. The first sharp in all sharp key signatures is *always* F, the second sharp is *always* C, the third G and so on. The first flat of all flat key signatures is *always* B, the second flat is *always* E, the third A and etc. Therefore, the circle of fifths, shown above, indicates that the key of G has 1♯ and that sharp must be F. The key of F is shown to have 1♭ and that flat must be B.

At the top of page 87 you will find not only the correct key signature notation but the specific order that the sharps and flats must follow.

Please note that the sharp and flat key signatures also follow the circle of fifths. The sharps begin at F (11 o'clock) and move clockwise to B (5 o'clock). The flats simply reverse the order and begin with B (5 o'clock) and move counterclockwise to F (11 o'clock).

In notating key signatures, the sharps or flats are placed on the staff in a certain pattern that is never altered in the treble clef, the first sharp, F, is always placed on the top line; in the bass clef, on the fourth line up. In the treble clef, the first flat, B, is always placed on the middle line; in the bass clef, on the second line up. The diagram on page 89 shows the placement of the remaining sharps and flats in the pattern that must always be followed. In notation, allow sufficient space so that none of the sharps or flats is directly above or below another.

F | C | G | D | A | E | B | | B | E | A | D | G | C | F

F | C | G | D | A | E | B | | B | E | A | D | G | C | F

3d Overtones

The use of the fifth in the circle of fifths is not an arbitrary choice. Every pitch is a composite of sounds, consisting of the main sound (the *fundamental*) plus many more. Most of these additional sounds, called **overtones**, **harmonics**, or **partials**, are not distinctly heard; however, the first overtone, which is an octave above the fundamental, and the second overtone, which is a fifth plus an octave over the fundamental, are clearly audible. This fifth is a very dominant sound for every pitch of the scale.

To hear these two overtones, *silently* depress the white keys of the piano from C to C with your right hand. With your left hand, strike the C one octave lower a hard, short blow. You will hear the tones C and G distinctly. Then silently depress the white keys from G to G, strike the G one octave lower, and you will hear G and D. You can continue this procedure throughout the circle of fifths.

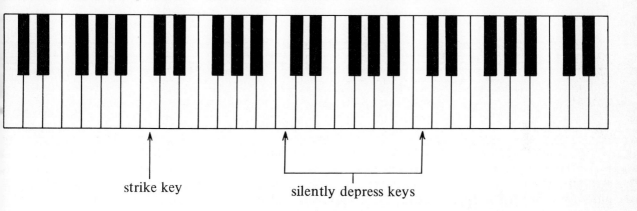

strike key   silently depress keys

The first seven overtones above the pitch C are shown below. This pattern of notes above the fundamental note—perfect octave, perfect fifth, perfect fourth, major third, and so forth—is called the *overtone series*, and it is duplicated above every pitch. The overtone series is the foundation for the circle of fifths, for the scales and chords of traditional harmony, and for the construction of contemporary Western musical instruments.

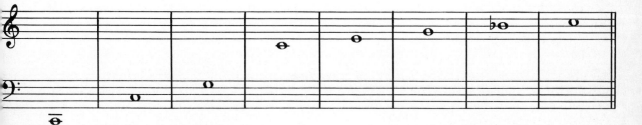

Major Scales with Sharps

Major Scales with Flats

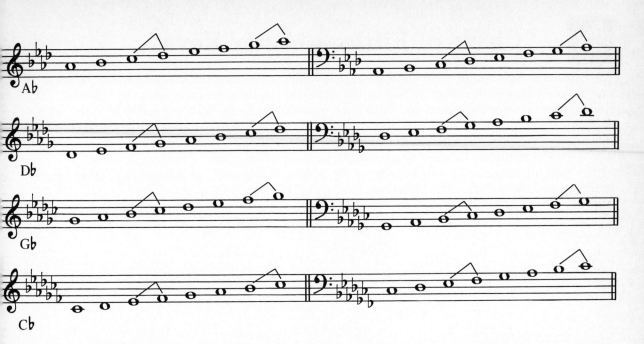

Another way to identify the key of the scale is to remember that in key signatures with sharps, the note one half step higher than the last sharp in the key signature gives the name of the key. In flat key signatures, the name of the next-to-last flat gives the name of the key.

3g Tetrachords

Another way to construct scales is by the use of the tetrachord, a concept that dates back to ancient Greek music. The **tetrachord** is a four-note pattern of whole steps and half steps that, when combined with another tetrachord, forms a one-octave scale. A *major tetrachord* is a pattern of two whole steps followed by a half step. Starting with C, an ascending series of this pattern, with each tetrachord separated by a whole step, will result in the twelve major scales, the last leading back to C. Any two neighboring tetrachords in this pattern will spell a major scale, as in the diagram below.

MAJOR-SCALE TETRACHORD SERIES

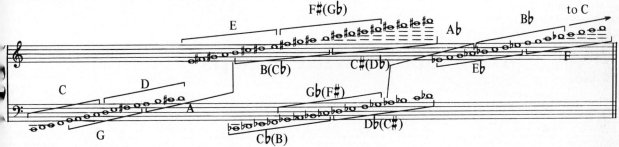

The minor scales and the modal scales (see 3n) can also be learned by memorizing their individual tetrachord patterns. Except for the Lydian mode, each tetrachord pattern will be separated by a whole step.

Major scale   1 2 3̂ 4 / 5 6 7̂ 8   Natural (unaltered) minor scale   1 2̂ 3 4 / 5̂ 6 7 8

Dorian mode   1 2̂ 3 4 / 5 6̂ 7 8   Phrygian mode   1̂ 2 3 4 / 5̂ 6 7 8

Lydian mode   1 2 3 4̂ / 5 6 7̂ 8   Mixolydian mode   1 2 3̂ 4 / 5 6̂ 7 8

3h Circle of Fifths—Minor Keys

The rules that apply to the major circle also apply to the circle in minor, as shown in the diagram below. The *natural* minor scale is represented by the white keys of the piano that span the octave A to A. Half steps appear between the second and third pitches, and between the fifth and sixth. With this whole-step and half-step pattern kept consistent by adding sharps or flats, the minor scale can be transposed to all the remaining eleven half steps within the octave. The scales requiring sharps are clockwise *ascending* fifths, and the scales requiring flats are counterclockwise *descending* fifths.

The natural minor scale can be altered by adding accidentals, to produce two other forms—the *harmonic* and the *melodic* minor (see 3k).

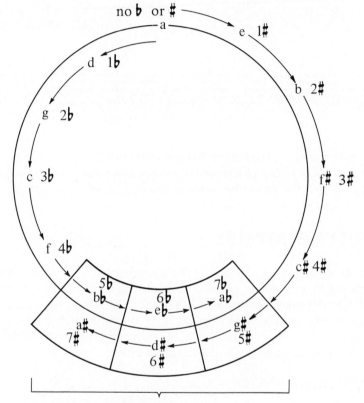

enharmonic keys

3i Minor Scales with Sharps

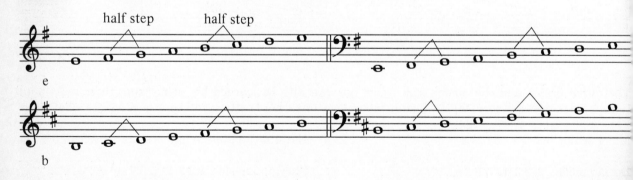

*The use of lowercase letters in this diagram to refer to minor keys is a well-known convention, and one this book will often use from now on. Thus capital G in diagrams means G major and lowercase g means g minor.

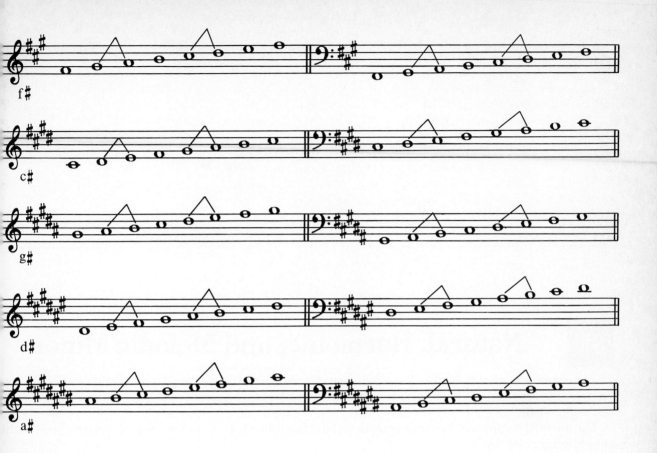

 ## Minor Scales with Flats

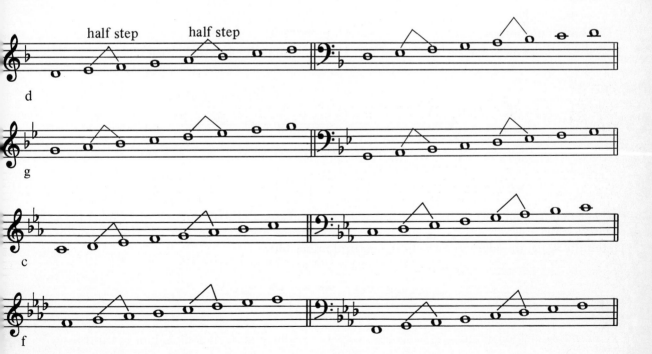

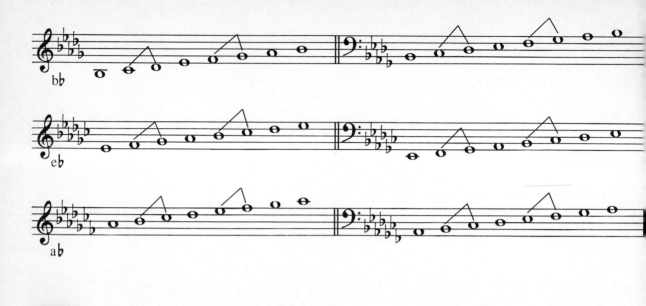

3k Natural, Harmonic, and Melodic Minor

The minor scale has three forms—the natural (unaltered) form, the harmonic form, and the melodic form. Each has its own unique characteristics. You should play and sing each form until you can recognize its distinct quality.

The **natural minor** scale is sometimes called the Aeolian minor, in reference to its origin as one of the church modes (see 3n).

natural minor

The **harmonic minor** scale raises the seventh pitch of the natural minor scale by one half step. This results in a skip of a step and a half between the sixth and seventh scale steps.

one and one-half steps

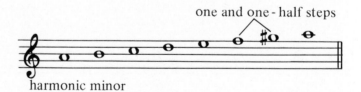

harmonic minor

The **ascending melodic minor** scale raises by one half step the sixth and seventh pitches of the natural minor scale. Descending, the sixth and seventh pitches are lowered one half step. The **descending melodic** scale, therefore, returns to the natural minor form.

ascending melodic minor   descending melodic minor (natural)

31 Relative Major and Minor

Major and minor keys with different names but with the same key signatures are called **relative**. To find the relative *minor* key of a major key, count down diatonically (by the steps in the scale) three pitches from the first note (the tonic) of the major scale, or count up, diatonically, six pitches from the tonic. To find the relative *major* key of a minor key, reverse the process: count down diatonically six pitches from the tonic, or count up three. In the following example, the key signature with one sharp applies to the keys of both G major and e minor.

F#   d#   Gb   eb

C#   a#   Cb   ab

3m   Parallel Major and Minor

Major and minor keys with different key signatures but with the same letter name and the same tonic are called **parallel**. The key signature of any parallel minor key is the same as that of its *relative* major. Find it by counting up three pitches diatonically from the minor tonic, a minor third, or by counting down six, a major sixth. Counting up three (minor third) or down six (major sixth) from G gives Bb, the relative major of g minor. Therefore two flats, the key signature of Bb, is also the key signature of g minor.

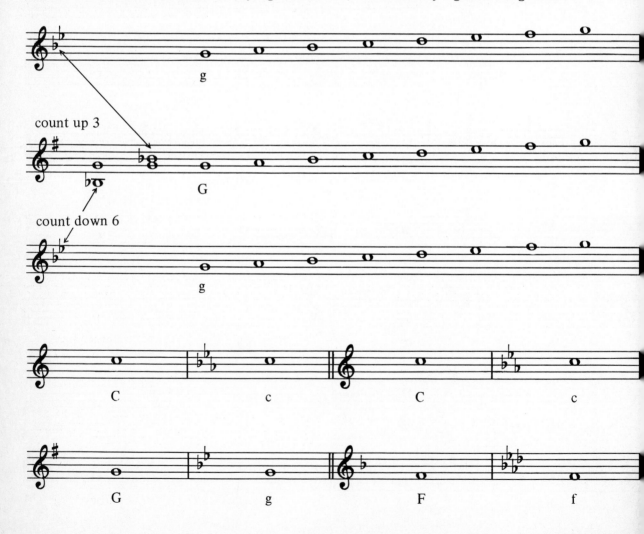

count up 3

g

G

count down 6

g

C   c   C   c

G   g   F   f

3n   The Church Modes

The **church modes** were the tonal basis of early music until roughly the end of the sixteenth century, the end of the Renaissance. The modes are octave segments of the C major scale, each placing the tonic on a different pitch in the scale (or white key on the piano). They appear on the staff as shown below. The major and minor scales replaced the modes and remained prominent until the nineteenth century, when composers rediscovered the early church modes and also became interested in other scale forms. The Dorian, Phrygian, Lydian, and Mixolydian modes remain in use today, the Dorian and Mixolydian being especially popular with composers of jazz and commercial music. An easy way to construct the modes is to think of them as either a major or minor scale with alterations, or as a major scale beginning and ending on a pitch other than tonic.

THE CHURCH MODES

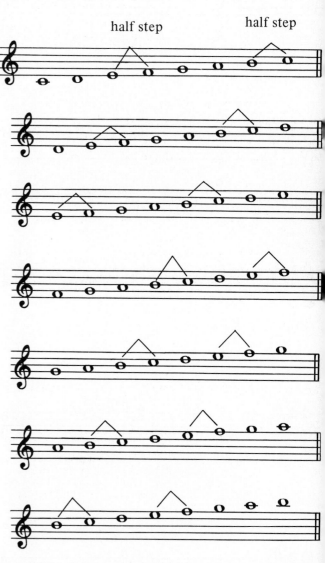

Ionian (major)

Dorian—a minor scale with a raised 6th or a Major scale played from the supertonic to supertonic.

Phrygian—a minor scale with a lowered 2nd or a Major scale played from the mediant to mediant.

Lydian—a Major scale with a raised 4th or a Major scale played from the subdominant to subdominant.

Mixolydian—a Major scale with a lowered 7th or a Major scale played from the dominant to dominant.

Aeolian (minor)

Locrian (very rare)—a minor scale with a lowered 2nd and 4th or a Major scale played from the "leading tone" to "leading tone."

Each mode may be transposed to any of the remaining half steps within the octave, and a circle of fifths can be established for each by following the same rules that apply to the major and minor scales. For example, the Dorian mode with no sharps or flats is called D Dorian. A fifth ascending is A Dorian, with the key signature of one sharp; a fifth descending is G Dorian, with the key signature of one flat. The modes may also be transposed by understanding and memorizing the tetrachord pattern for each (see 3g).

30 Other Scale Forms

Many other forms of scales can be found in music, including Near Eastern and Oriental scales that do not use the half-step and whole-step patterns, scales unique to an ethnic or regional group, and original or "created" scales that are created by the composer for a specific effect.

The pentatonic scale, a scale with only five different pitches (in contrast to the seven pitches of the major and minor scales), can be easily played on the piano by using the black keys only. This scale occurred in China as early as 2000 B.C.

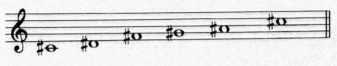

pentatonic scale

The whole-tone scale, a six-tone scale beginning on C, can only be transposed once, to C♯. This scale was exploited by the French Impressionist composers of the late nineteenth century because it lacks a feeling of tonic; it thus creates a vagueness of tonality or key.

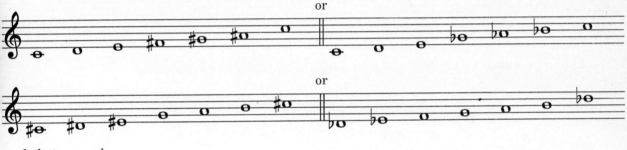

whole-tone scale

The following scale is but one of many that could be created by a composer.

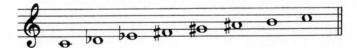

original (synthetic) scale

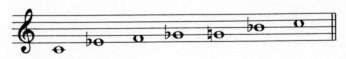

a "pop blues" scale

The Chromatic Scale

When any nondiatonic tones (see 3b) are introduced into a scale, they are called *chromatic* tones. The introduction of every chromatic tone results in the **chromatic scale**, all the twelve tones within an octave. In general, sharps are used to notate the ascending scale; flats notate the descending scale, but sharps or flats found in the key signature should be accounted for. Below is the *c* ascending and descending chromatic scale, also the *F* ascending chromatic scale and the G descending chromatic scale.

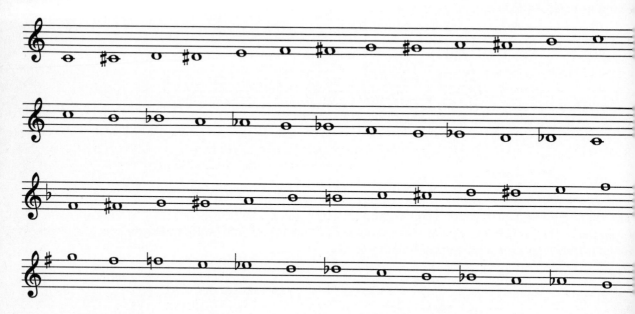

The white-key half-step pairs (E-F and B-C) are always notated as natural notes.

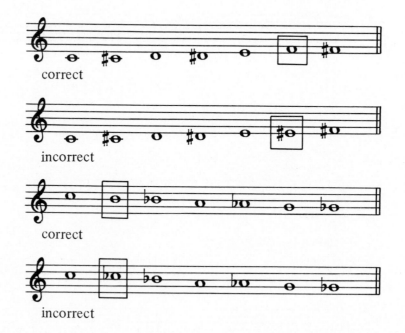

correct

incorrect

correct

incorrect

3q Twelve-Tone Rows

In the early twentieth century, the composer Arnold Schoenberg (1874–1951) devised a pitch system to replace the traditional melodic, tonal, and chordal relationships of the music of the eighteenth and nineteenth centuries. A composition using this sytem is based on an arrangement of all twelve chromatic tones into a series, or **twelve-tone row**. The series usually remains unaltered throughout a work except for the modifications listed below. The composing of a series and its creative use is an advanced and complex skill, but the basic rules can be understood by the beginning theory student:

1. The row can be used in four forms:
   O—in the original form
   I—in inversion (upside down, with each interval inverted)
   R—in retrograde (backward)
   RI—in retrograde inversion (backward and upside down)
2. These four forms can be transposed to any step of the chromatic scale, allowing a possible total of 48 versions of the original row.
3. From this basic material, melodic progressions and chordal combinations can be formed. The twelve tones are usually presented in full, arranged horizontally or vertically, before the series, in any of its forms, is repeated.
4. Any range, clef, skip, repetition of tones, simultaneous use of tones, octave position of tones, or enharmonic spelling of tones is allowed.
5. Once the row is started, the pre-established note sequence is followed through all the twelve notes of the row. You do not randomly pick notes from the row.

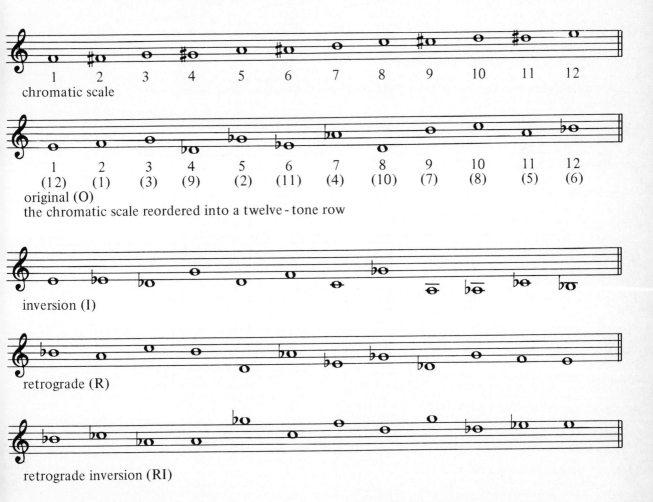

chromatic scale

original (O)
the chromatic scale reordered into a twelve - tone row

inversion (I)

retrograde (R)

retrograde inversion (RI)

Here is part of a melody using the inverted form of the row.

Schoenberg

SCHOENBERG, WALTZ, OP. 23, NO. 5

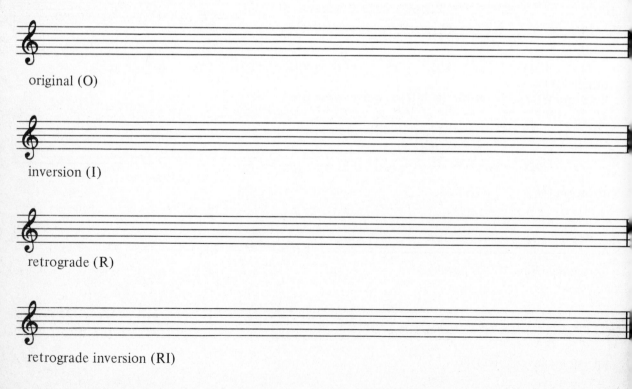

Arrange the twelve chromatic tones into your own twelve-tone row, then construct its remaining three forms.

original (O)

inversion (I)

retrograde (R)

retrograde inversion (RI)

Worksheet 3-1

Name the major keys and write the tonic on the staff for the following key signatures. If possible, without leger lines, write the tonic in two different octaves.

3e

3f

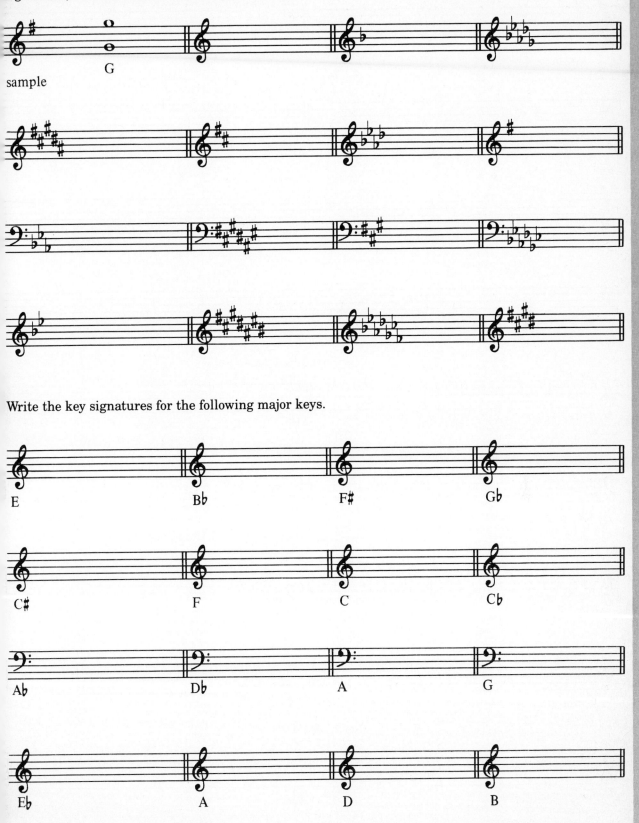

sample G

Write the key signatures for the following major keys.

E   Bb   F#   Gb

C#   F   C   Cb

Ab   Db   A   G

Eb   A   D   B

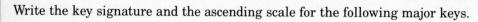
3e
3f

Write the key signature and the ascending scale for the following major keys.

C   A

Db   G

D   Cb

F   A

E   Bb

Eb   B

F♯   Ab

E   C♯

Gb   Eb

Worksheet 3-3

Name the minor keys and write the tonic on the staff for the following key signatures. If possible, without leger lines, write the tonic in two different octaves.

3**i**

3**j**

Write the key signatures for the following minor keys.

d♯   g   b   a♭

a♯   e   c   g♯

a   b♭   e♭   a♯

d   c♯   f   f♯

Worksheet 3-4

3i
3j

Write the key signature and the ascending scale for the following minor keys. Use the natural form.

g

b

c

d

a

f#

f

d#

g#

a#

e

c

ab

bb

f#

bb

eb

c#

Worksheet 3-5

Write the *relative* minor scales for the following major scales in all forms as indicated.

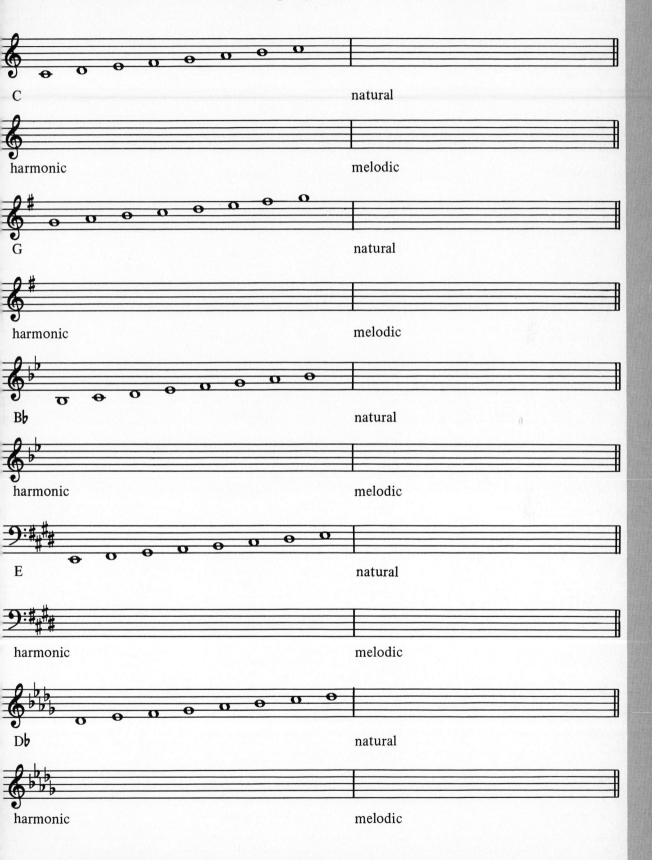

C   natural

harmonic   melodic

G   natural

harmonic   melodic

B♭   natural

harmonic   melodic

E   natural

harmonic   melodic

D♭   natural

harmonic   melodic

Worksheet 3-6

Using the proper key signatures, write the *parallel* minor scales for the following major scales in all forms as indicated.

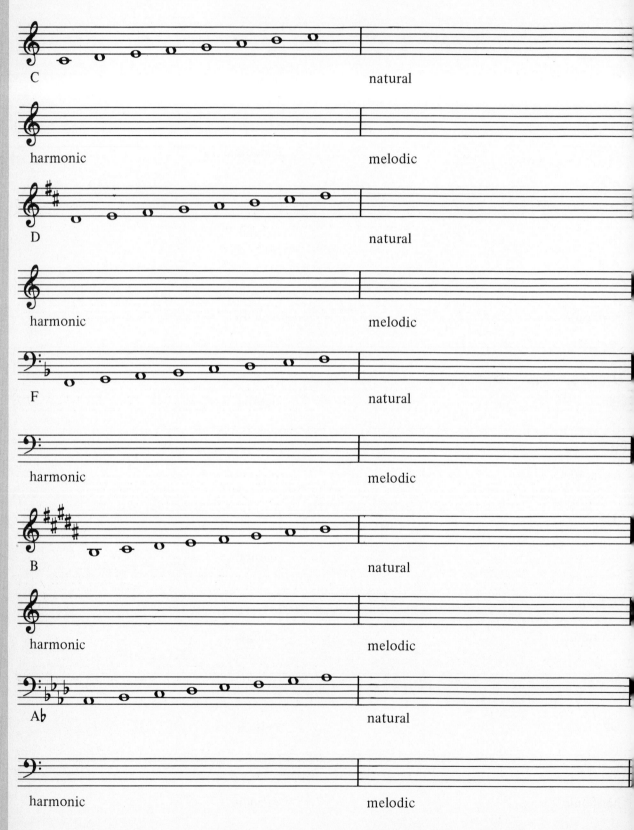

C   natural

harmonic   melodic

D   natural

harmonic   melodic

F   natural

harmonic   melodic

B   natural

harmonic   melodic

A♭   natural

harmonic   melodic

Write key signatures and *ascending* scales as indicated. For minor scales, use the harmonic form.

parallel major of f

relative major of e

parallel minor of B

relative minor of F

parallel minor of D

relative major of d

parallel minor of E

relative minor of E♭

relative major of g♯

parallel major of e♭

relative minor of A♭

relative major of b♭

parallel minor of B♭

relative minor of B

parallel minor of D♭

relative major of f♯

parallel major of a♭

parallel major of b

Worksheet 3-8

Write key signatures and *ascending* scales as indicated. For melodic minor scales write only the ascending scale.

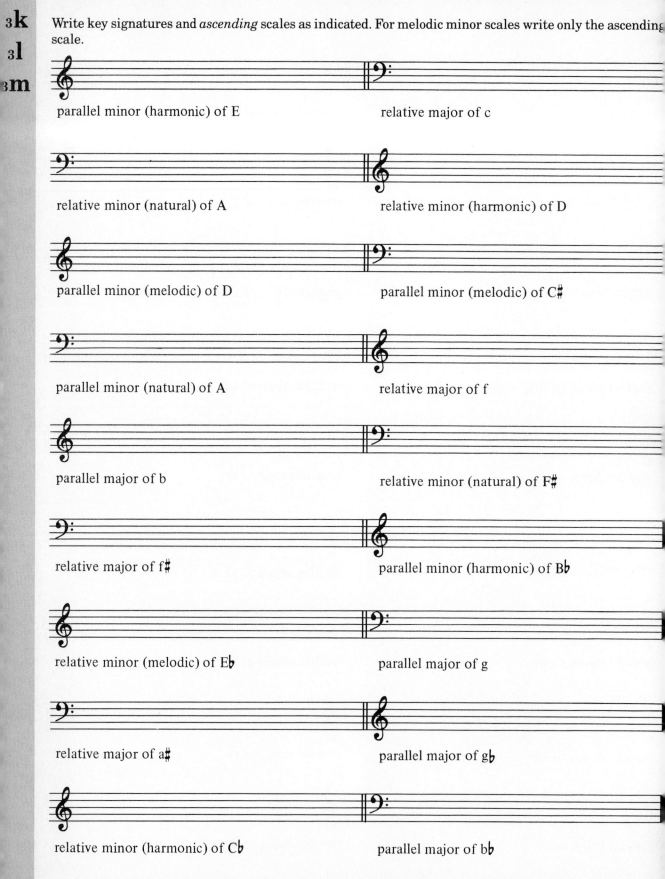

parallel minor (harmonic) of E

relative major of c

relative minor (natural) of A

relative minor (harmonic) of D

parallel minor (melodic) of D

parallel minor (melodic) of C♯

parallel minor (natural) of A

relative major of f

parallel major of b

relative minor (natural) of F♯

relative major of f♯

parallel minor (harmonic) of B♭

relative minor (melodic) of E♭

parallel major of g

relative major of a♯

parallel major of g♭

relative minor (harmonic) of C♭

parallel major of b♭

Worksheet 3-9

Write key signatures and *ascending* scales as indicated. For melodic minor scales write only the ascending scale.

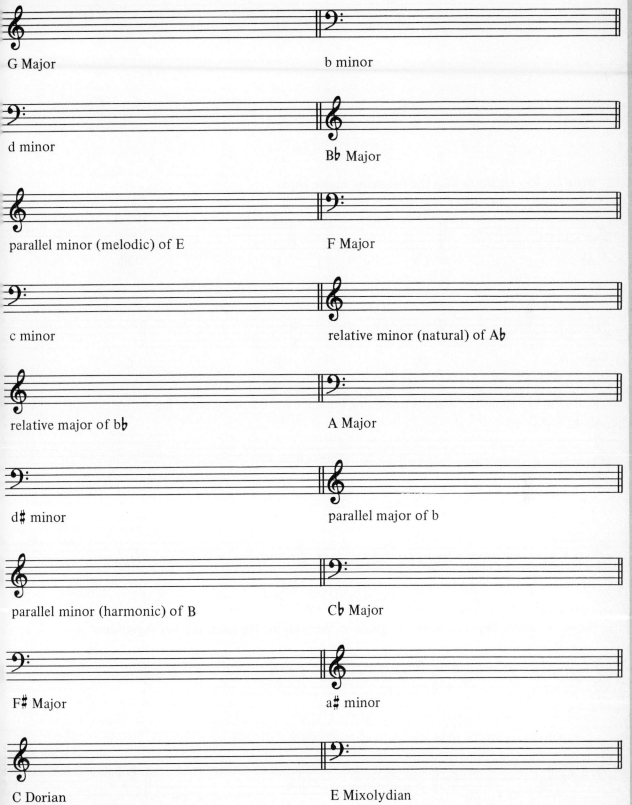

G Major

b minor

d minor

B♭ Major

parallel minor (melodic) of E

F Major

c minor

relative minor (natural) of A♭

relative major of b♭

A Major

d♯ minor

parallel major of b

parallel minor (harmonic) of B

C♭ Major

F♯ Major

a♯ minor

C Dorian

E Mixolydian

3k
3l
3m
3n

3e
3f

1. Name the major keys and write the tonic on the staff for the following key signatures.

3e
3f

2. Write the key signatures for the following major keys.

Ab　　　　Cb　　　　D　　　　Bb

B　　　　F#　　　　F　　　　G

3e
3f

3. Write the key signature and the ascending scale for the following major keys.

F　　　　A

Db　　　　F#

3i
3j

4. Name the minor keys and write the tonic on the staff for the following key signatures.

112

5. Write the key signatures for the following minor keys.

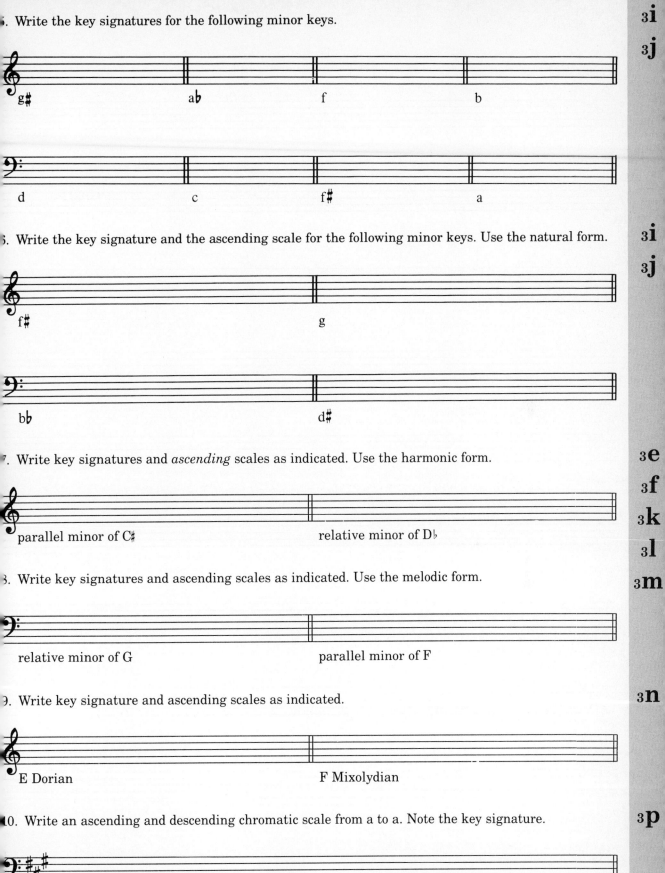

g#   ab   f   b

d   c   f#   a

6. Write the key signature and the ascending scale for the following minor keys. Use the natural form.

f#   g

bb   d#

7. Write key signatures and *ascending* scales as indicated. Use the harmonic form.

parallel minor of C#   relative minor of Db

8. Write key signatures and ascending scales as indicated. Use the melodic form.

relative minor of G   parallel minor of F

9. Write key signature and ascending scales as indicated.

E Dorian   F Mixolydian

10. Write an ascending and descending chromatic scale from a to a. Note the key signature.

113

Intervals

4a   Constructing Intervals

An **interval** is the distance between two tones. All intervals have two components—*number size* and *quality*. The number size of an interval is calculated by counting the total number of letter names between and including the two tones, either up or down, as in the examples below. **Be sure to count the starting note as "one" when calculating an interval.**

C-D includes only two letters of the alphabet, C and D, so the interval is a second.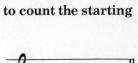

F-D (counting down) includes three letters of the alphabet, F, E, and D, so the interval is a third.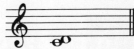

A-G includes seven letters of the alphabet, A, B, C, D, E, F, and G, so the interval is a seventh.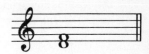

The quality of an interval is its distinctive sound. The interval of a second, for example, always includes two tones, but it is the number of half steps or whole steps between the two that dictates its quality. C-D♭♭, C-D♭, C-D, C-D♯, and C-D× are all diatonic seconds, but each sounds different—each has its own unique quality.

4b   Perfect and Major Intervals

Within a major diatonic scale, there are four perfect and four major intervals above the tonic of that scale. In the following example, the perfect and major intervals are named from C, the root (or lowest tone) in the scale of C major. In identifying the perfect and major intervals in other major keys, be sure to keep in mind the sharps or flats in the key signature.

The perfect intervals (unison, fourth, fifth, and octave) are called "perfect" because they are overtones that are closely connected to the fundamental tone (see 3d). The early development of scales was based on the interval of the fifth—the ascending fifth (C-G, G-D, etc.) and the descending fifth (C-F, the pitch a fifth below C). Although the unison—*perfect prime*—cannot be counted by a total of letter names between the two tones, it is nevertheless an interval.

The major intervals are the second, third, sixth, and seventh. *Major* means "larger," as opposed to *minor*, which means "smaller."

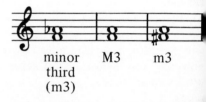

| perfect unison or perfect prime (P1) | major second (M2) | major third (M3) | perfect fourth (P4) | perfect fifth (P5) | major sixth (M6) | major seventh (M7) | perfect octave (P8) |

 ## 4c   Minor Intervals

A major interval made one half step smaller becomes a **minor** interval. The top tone is lowered one half step, or the bottom tone is raised one half step. Changing minor to major is the reverse.

minor third (m3)   M3   m3

4d   Diminished and Augmented Intervals

A minor interval made one half step smaller becomes diminished. The top tone is lowered one half step or the bottom tone raised one half step. Diminished to minor is the reverse.

diminished third (d3)   m3   d3

(*Rare:* A diminished interval made one half step smaller becomes doubly diminished. The top tone is lowered one half step or the bottom tone is raised one half step. Doubly diminished to diminished is the reverse.)

dd3   d3   dd3

A perfect interval made one half step smaller becomes diminished. The top tone is lowered one half step or the bottom tone raised one half step. Diminished to perfect is the reverse.

d4   P4   d4

A perfect interval or major interval made one half step larger becomes **augmented**. The top tone is raised one half step or the bottom tone lowered one half step. Augmented to perfect or major is the reverse.

augmented fourth (A4)   P4   A4

Rare: An augmented interval made one half step larger becomes doubly augmented. The top tone is raised one half step or the bottom one lowered one half step. Doubly augmented to augmented is the reverse.)

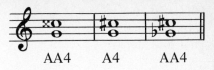

AA4   A4   AA4

Perfect Intervals 1-4-5-8	one half step smaller = d
	one half step larger = A

Major Intervals 2-3-6-7	one half step smaller = m
	two half steps smaller = d
	one half step larger = A

*P = Perfect
M = Major
m = minor
d = diminished
A = Augmented

4e   Constructing Intervals—Another Method

Besides the number of letter names between the two tones, intervals can be identified and constructed by the number of whole and half steps they encompass. For the major second and third, and for the perfect fourth and fifth, memorize the number of whole and half steps above or below a given tone, as shown below. For the major sixth and seventh, memorize the number of whole and half steps *less than an octave* that each contains. For example, an octave above C is C; one diatonic half step below C is B. So B is a major seventh above C. Or an octave *below* C is C; one diatonic half step above that C is D♭, a major seventh below C. Once you identify the major or perfect interval, you can alter it to minor, diminished, or augmented by the methods described in section 4d.

In this method of interval construction, you must make sure to observe the correct diatonic note spelling. For example, a major third above D (D-E-F) is F♯, not G♭ (D-E-F-G is a fourth).

unison

or

M2
one whole step
(two half steps)

or

*Uppercase letters are used for Major, Perfect, and Augmented intervals and lowercase letters are used for minor and diminished intervals.

M3
two whole steps
(four half steps)

P4
two and one-half steps

P5
three and one-half steps

M6
one and one-half steps *less* than an octave

M7
one half step *less* than an octave

P8
octave

4f   Simple and Compound Intervals

A simple interval is an interval of an octave or less. A compound interval is an interval greater than an octave. It is easier and more convenient to reduce the compound interval to a simple interval plus an octave. Subtract seven from the compound number and it will give you a quick simple interval pitch.

> 7 from 10 is a third, a third plus an octave equals a 10th.
> 7 from 12 is a fifth, a fifth plus an octave equals a 12th.

The terms Major and Perfect also apply to the compound intervals. An 11th is a 4th plus an octave and is called a perfect 11th. A 13th is a 6th plus an octave and is called a Major 13th.

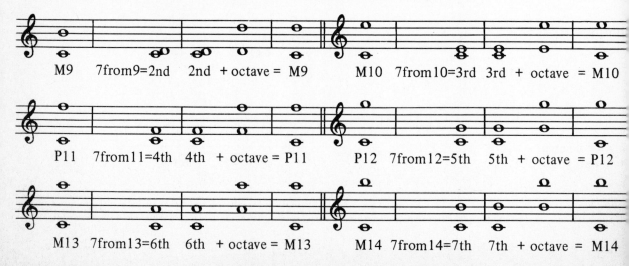

M9   7from9=2nd   2nd + octave = M9   M10   7from10=3rd   3rd + octave = M10

P11   7from11=4th   4th + octave = P11   P12   7from12=5th   5th + octave = P12

M13   7from13=6th   6th + octave = M13   M14   7from14=7th   7th + octave = M14

4g   The Tritone

When all the fourths of the major scale are arranged in order, the one built on the fourth degree of the scale is one half step larger than a perfect fourth; therefore, it is augmented. The augmented fourth contains *three whole steps*, so it is called the **tritone**, meaning "three tones." As a melodic progression, the tritone sounds awkward. In early music it was forbidden, and was referred to as "the devil in music." In certain contexts, including student work, the rule prohibiting the melodic tritone is still observed.

4h   Constructing Intervals Downward

There are three methods of constructing an interval below a given tone, all of which apply to compound as well as simple intervals:

1. by counting whole steps and half steps (already described in section 4e)
2. by identification and alteration
3. by interval inversion

(1) METHOD 1   COUNTING BY WHOLE AND HALF STEPS

See section 4e for a description of this method.

(2) METHOD 2   IDENTIFICATION AND ALTERATION

Count down the correct number of letter names without considering accidentals. Then from the bottom tone identify the quality of the interval and, if necessary, alter the bottom tone to produce the desired interval. (Remember: *lowering* the bottom tone makes an interval larger; *raising* the bottom tone makes an interval smaller.)

For example: what is a major sixth below C? E is the sixth pitch below C. E-C is identified from the bottom tone as a minor sixth. Therefore, the E must be altered *down* by a half step to E♭. The interval is now a major sixth.

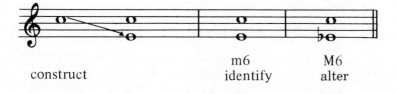

construct   m6   M6
                   identify   alter

(3) METHOD 3   BY INTERVAL INVERSION

If you are at ease finding intervals above a note you may find intervals below a given note by following a few simple rules. (1) Remember that an *inverted* interval adds up to *nine*—a third above C is E and a sixth below C is E. (2) In inversion the quality of the interval changes from Major ↔ minor, Augmented ↔ diminished, and Perfect ↔ Perfect. For example, what is a minor third below A? A Major sixth *above* A is F♯; therefore, a minor third below A is also F♯.

1. An interval and its inversion will always add up to *nine*.
   A second inverted is a seventh.
   A third inverted is a sixth.
   A fourth inverted is a fifth.
   A fifth inverted is a fourth.
   A sixth inverted is a third.
   A seventh inverted is a second.
2. The quality of an interval will change when it is inverted, with the exception of the perfect intervals.
   A major interval inverted is a minor.
   A minor interval inverted is a major.
   A perfect interval inverted remains perfect.
   A diminished interval inverted is augmented.
   An augmented interval inverted is diminished.

INVERSION OF INTERVALS

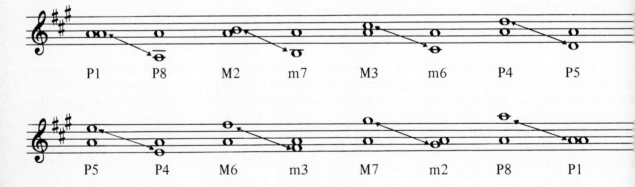

Complete the following by adding major seconds *above* the given notes.*

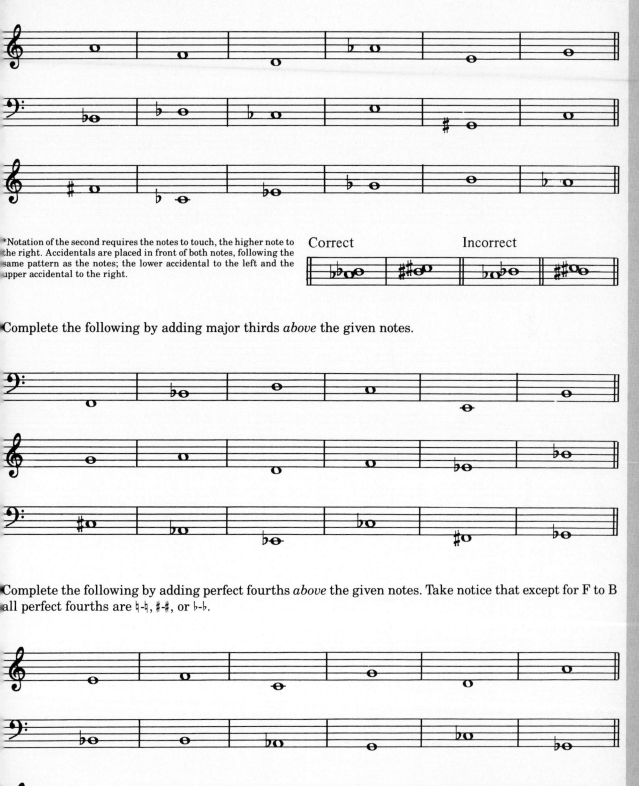

*Notation of the second requires the notes to touch, the higher note to the right. Accidentals are placed in front of both notes, following the same pattern as the notes; the lower accidental to the left and the upper accidental to the right.

Correct   Incorrect

Complete the following by adding major thirds *above* the given notes.

Complete the following by adding perfect fourths *above* the given notes. Take notice that except for F to B all perfect fourths are ♮-♮, ♯-♯, or ♭-♭.

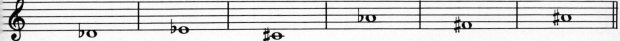

4b Complete the following by adding perfect fifths *above* the given notes. Take notice that except for B to F all perfect fifths are ♮-♮, ♯-♯, or ♭-♭.

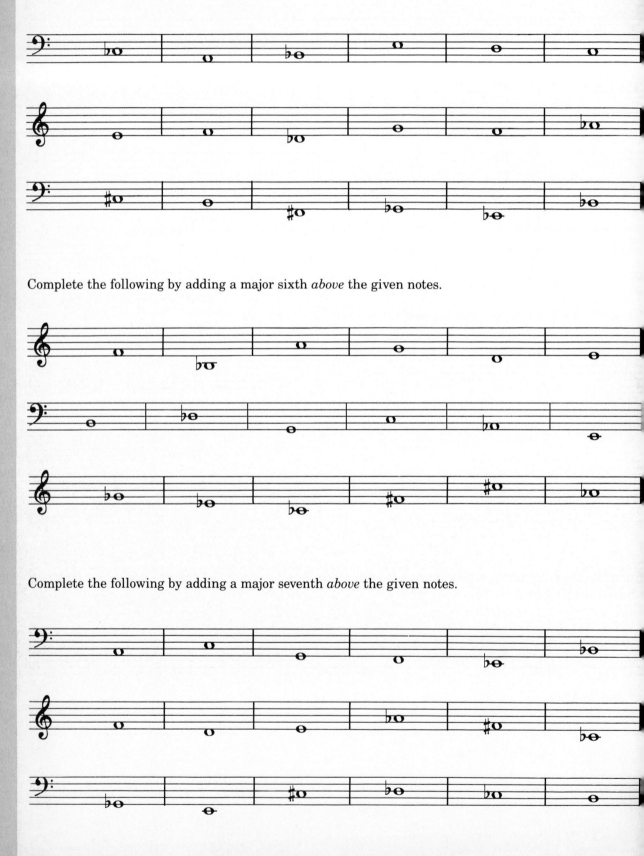

Complete the following by adding a major sixth *above* the given notes.

Complete the following by adding a major seventh *above* the given notes.

Worksheet 4-3

NAME _____

Complete the following intervals by adding a note *above* the given note.

4b

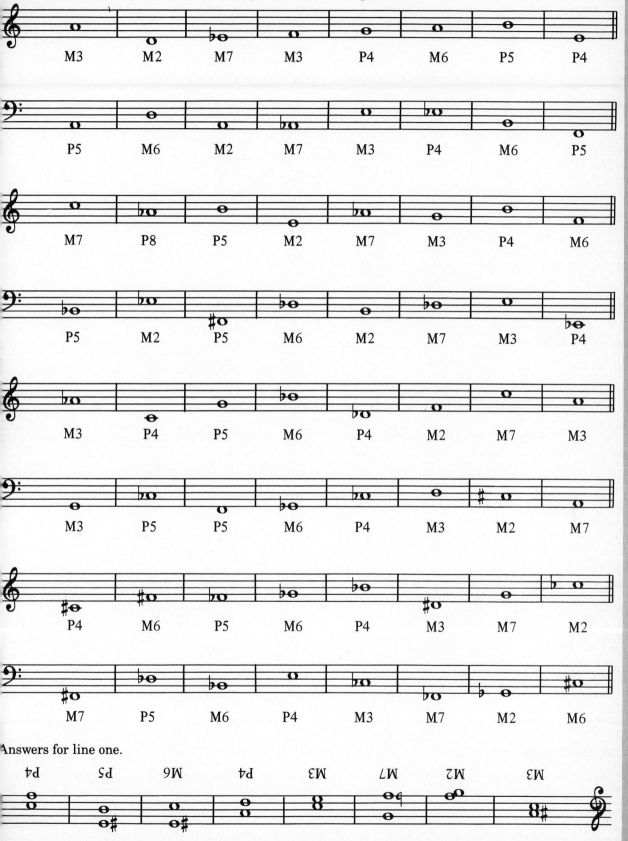

Answers for line one.

Complete the following intervals by adding a note *above* the given note.

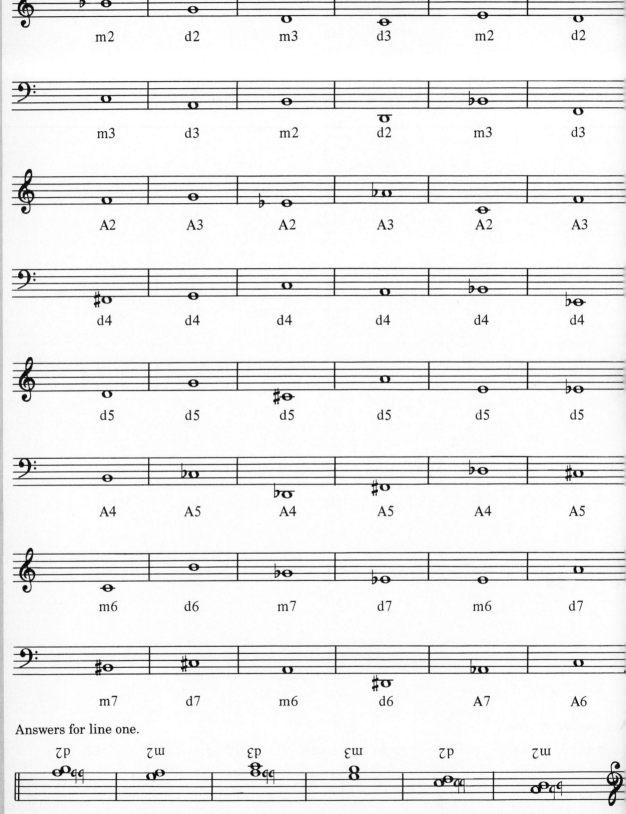

4c

4d

Answers for line one.

Complete the following intervals by adding a note *above* the given note.

4b

4c

4d

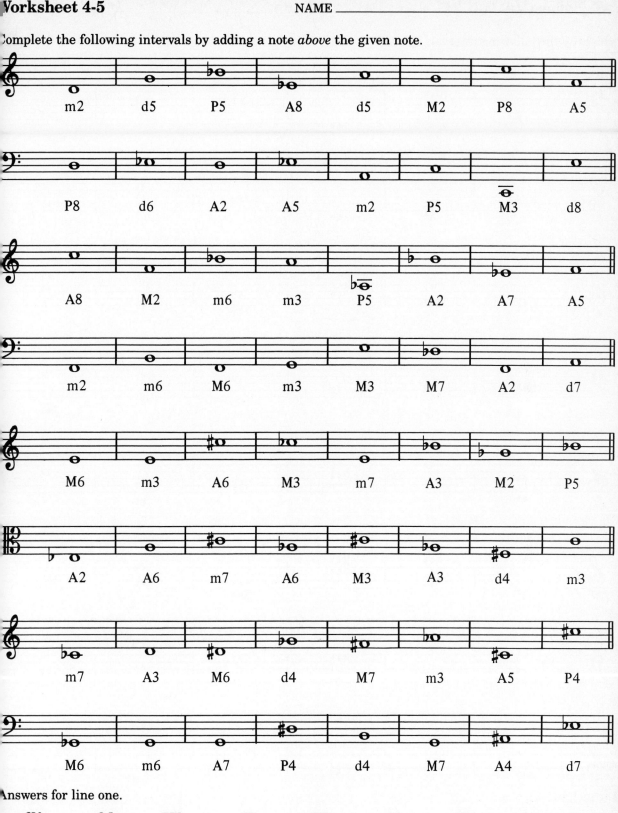

m2   d5   P5   A8   d5   M2   P8   A5

P8   d6   A2   A5   m2   P5   M3   d8

A8   M2   m6   m3   P5   A2   A7   A5

m2   m6   M6   m3   M3   M7   A2   d7

M6   m3   A6   M3   m7   A3   M2   P5

A2   A6   m7   A6   M3   A3   d4   m3

m7   A3   M6   d4   M7   m3   A5   P4

M6   m6   A7   P4   d4   M7   A4   d7

Answers for line one.

Worksheet 4-6

4b
4c
4d

Identify the following intervals by number and quality using the abbreviations P, M, m, d, or A.

NAME _____

Identify the following intervals by number and quality using the abbreviations P, M, m, d, or A.

4h Complete the following by adding major seconds *below* the given notes.

Complete the following by adding a major third *below* the given note.

Complete the following by adding a perfect fourth *below* the given note. Take notice that except for B to all perfect fourths are ♮-♮, #-#, or ♭-♭.

NAME _____

Complete the following by adding perfect fifths *below* the given notes. Take notice that except for F to B all perfect fifths are ♮-♮, ♯-♯, or ♭-♭.

4h

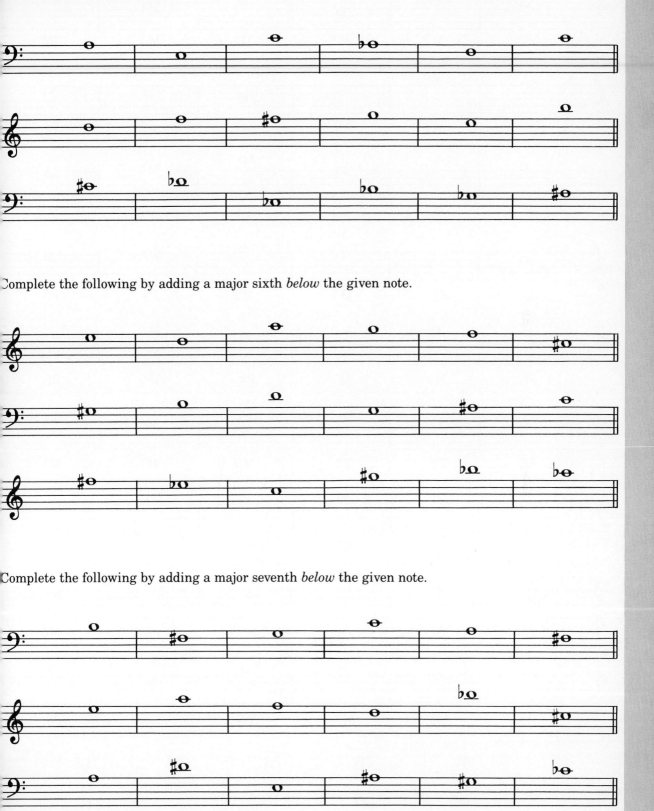

Complete the following by adding a major sixth *below* the given note.

Complete the following by adding a major seventh *below* the given note.

129

Worksheet 4-10 NAME _____

4h

Complete the following intervals by adding a note *below* the given note.

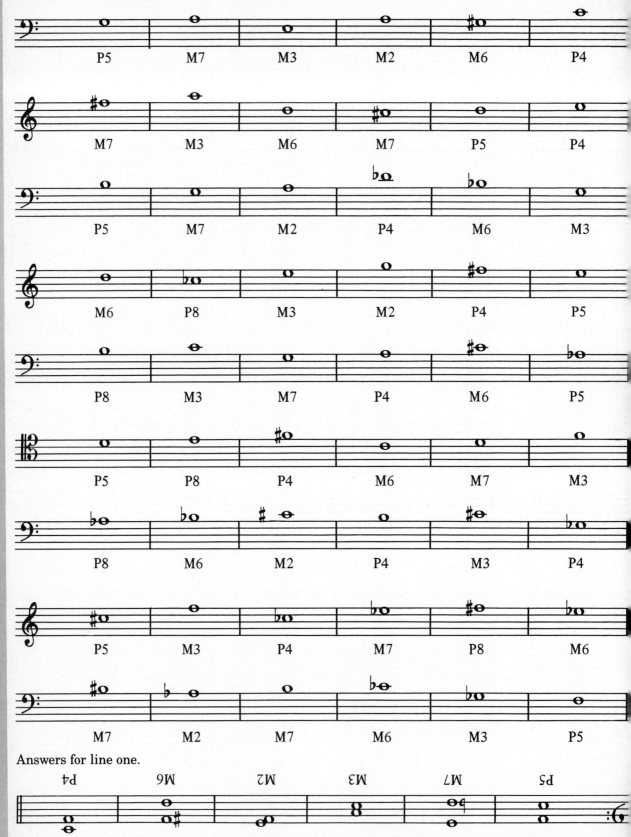

Answers for line one.

Worksheet 4-11

Complete the following intervals by adding a note *below* the given note.

Answers for line one.

Worksheet 4-12

Complete the following intervals by adding a note *below* the given note.

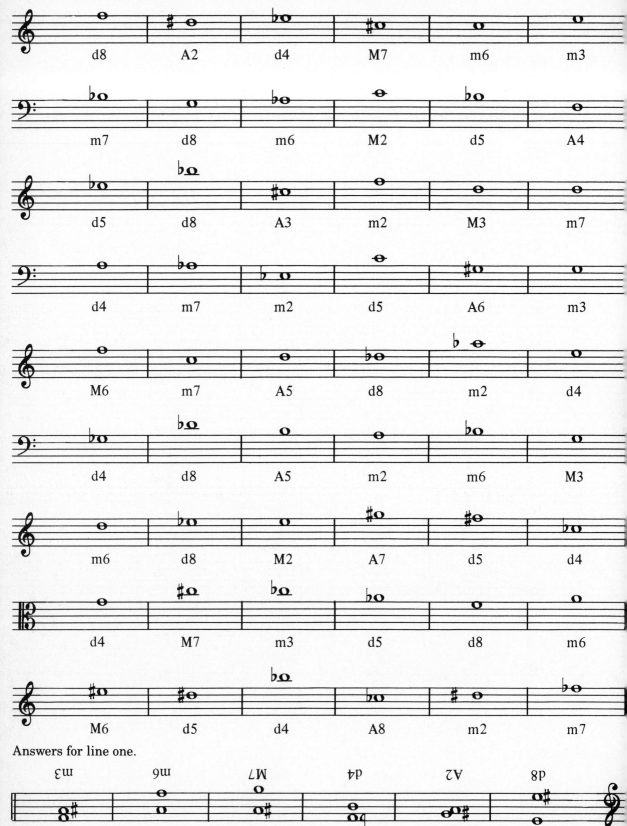

Answers for line one.

Worksheet 4-13

Complete the following compound intervals by adding a note *above* the given note.

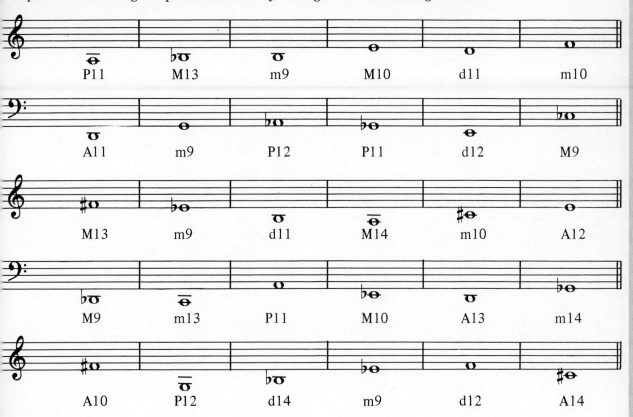

P11   M13   m9   M10   d11   m10

A11   m9   P12   P11   d12   M9

M13   m9   d11   M14   m10   A12

M9   m13   P11   M10   A13   m14

A10   P12   d14   m9   d12   A14

Complete the following compound intervals by adding a note *below* the given note.

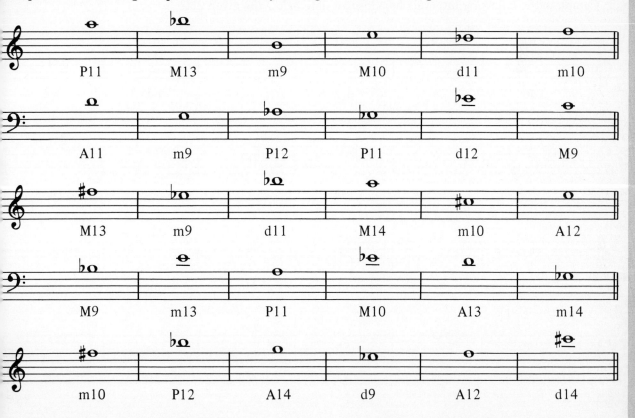

P11   M13   m9   M10   d11   m10

A11   m9   P12   P11   d12   M9

M13   m9   d11   M14   m10   A12

M9   m13   P11   M10   A13   m14

m10   P12   A14   d9   A12   d14

1. Complete the following intervals by adding a note *above* the given note.

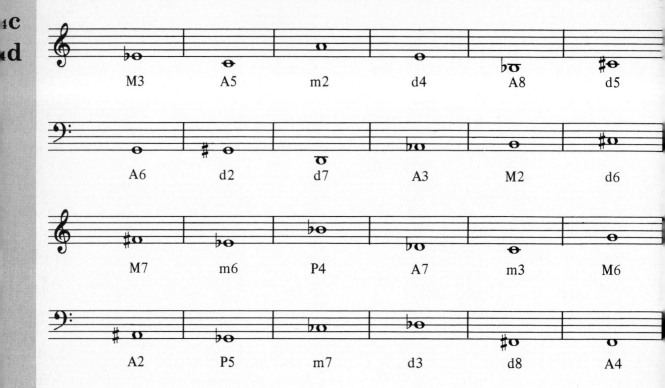

2. Complete the following intervals by adding a note *below* the given note.

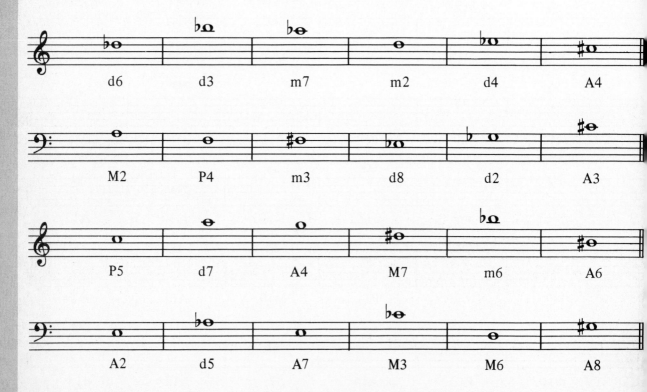

3. Identify the following intervals by number and quality using the abbreviations P, M, m, d, or A.

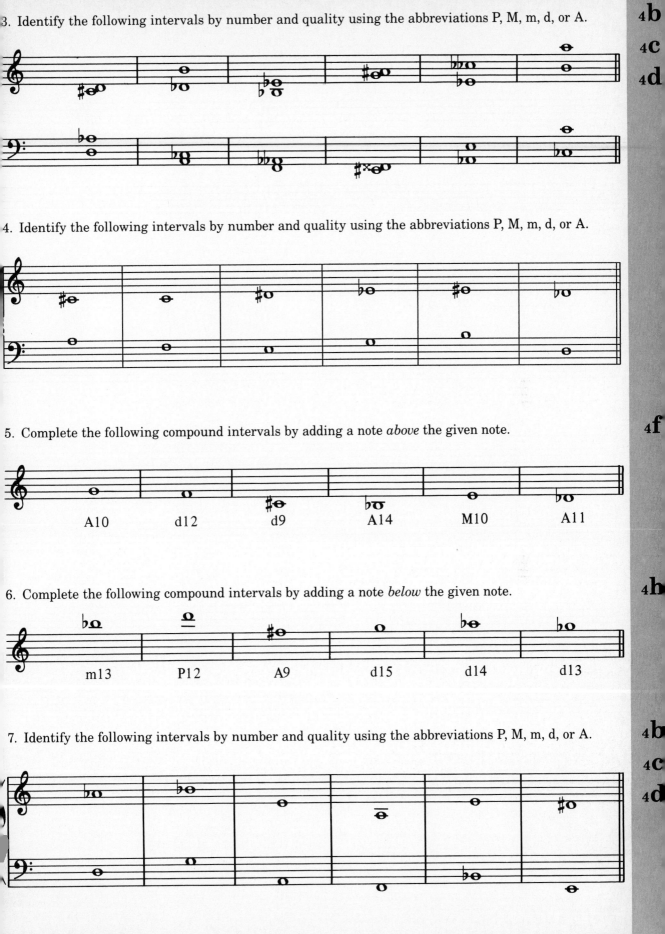

4. Identify the following intervals by number and quality using the abbreviations P, M, m, d, or A.

5. Complete the following compound intervals by adding a note *above* the given note.

A10   d12   d9   A14   M10   A11

6. Complete the following compound intervals by adding a note *below* the given note.

m13   P12   A9   d15   d14   d13

7. Identify the following intervals by number and quality using the abbreviations P, M, m, d, or A.

5

Rhythmic and Melodic Exercises—Intermediate

Before performing the rhythmic exercises in this unit, review the rules of good practice habits (2a); review also compound meter signatures (1f). Compound meters involve rhythmic groupings of three beats or divisions of a beat into three equal parts, and may be counted in either of the following ways: count the division values as *1* 2 3, *4* 5 6 (*7* 8 9, *10* 11 12) with an accent on 1, 4 (7, 10); or let the sounds "eh" and "ah" represent the second and third division of each group of three—*1*-eh-ah, *2*-eh-ah, (*3*-eh-ah, *4*-eh-ah). Both methods have their advantages. Try each method several times and use the one that feels best.

Compound meter signatures convey the feeling of skipping (*long*-short, *long*-short), or of a waltz (1-2-3, 1-2-3), or of a word or words (*pine*apple, *riv*erboat, *Lud*wig van *Bee*thoven). Try to develop a feeling for each meter signature and its characteristic divisions and subdivisions. A simple word pattern or familiar tune may be very helpful in establishing that unique feeling for a particular meter.

5a   Rhythmic Exercises

(1) COMPOUND METERS WITH BEAT DIVISION

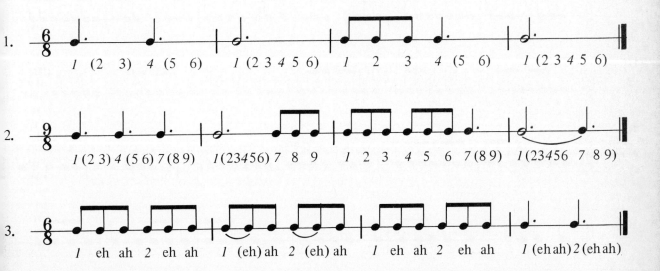

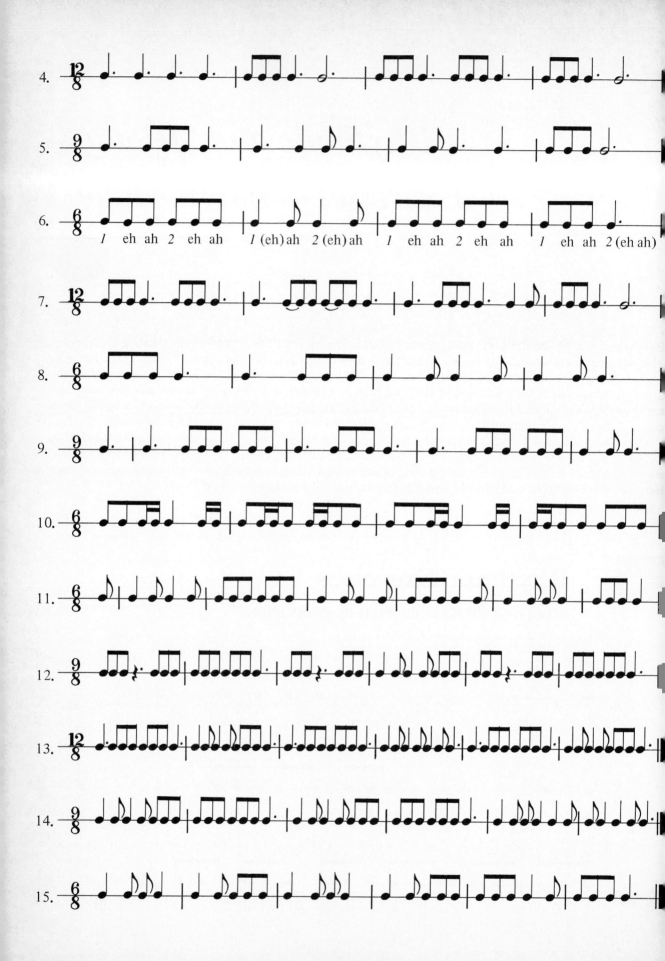

138

(2) EIGHT-MEASURE EXERCISES

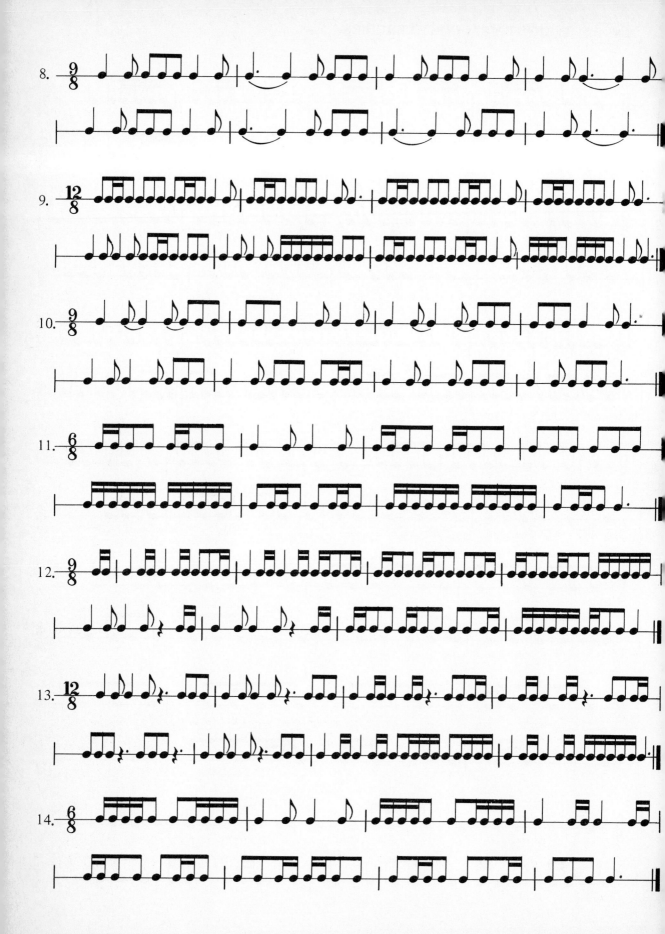

(3) COORDINATED-SKILL EXERCISES

141

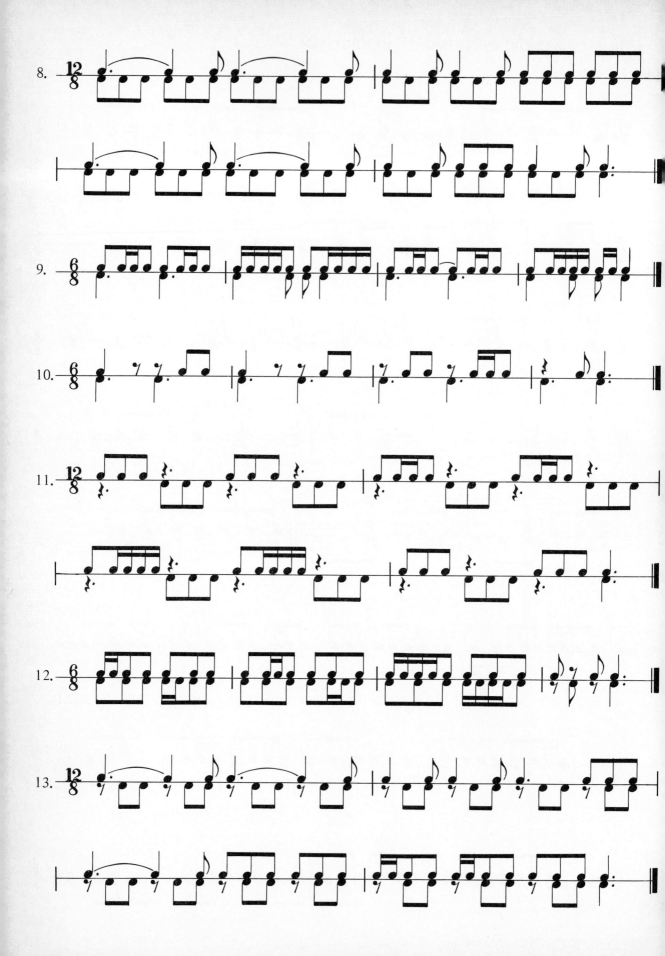

(4) NEW MATERIAL DOTTED NOTES ♪. AND ♪.

For an accurate performance of the dotted eighth and sixteenth (♪.♪ or ♩.♪), and the dotted sixteenth and 32nd (♪.♪ or ♩.♪), count the subdivision of the beat, tapping the note on the appropriate word.

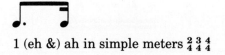

1 (eh &) ah in simple meters $\frac{2}{4}$ $\frac{3}{4}$ $\frac{4}{4}$

1 (eh &) ah in simple meters $\frac{2}{8}$ $\frac{3}{8}$ $\frac{4}{8}$

1 (2) & 3 4 (5) & 6 in compound meters $\frac{6}{8}$ $\frac{9}{8}$ $\frac{12}{8}$

144

(5) EIGHT-MEASURE EXERCISES

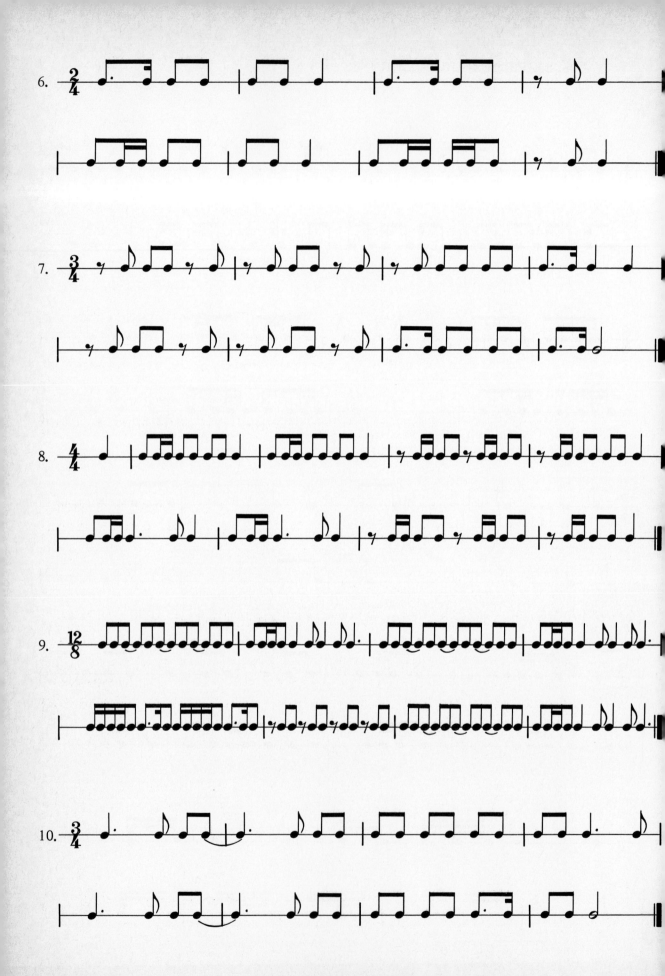

(6) COORDINATED-SKILL EXERCISES

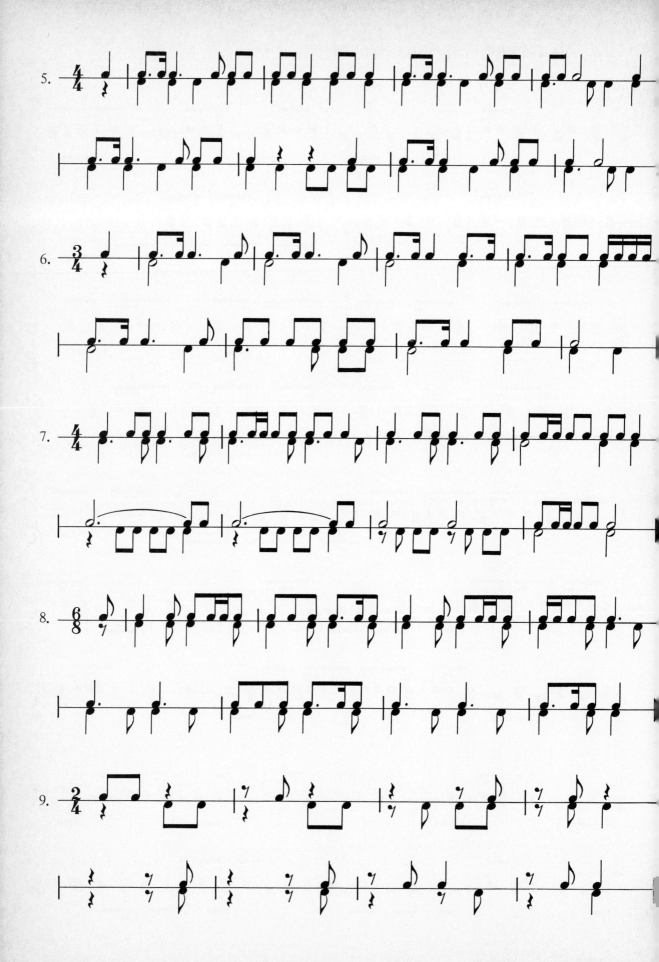

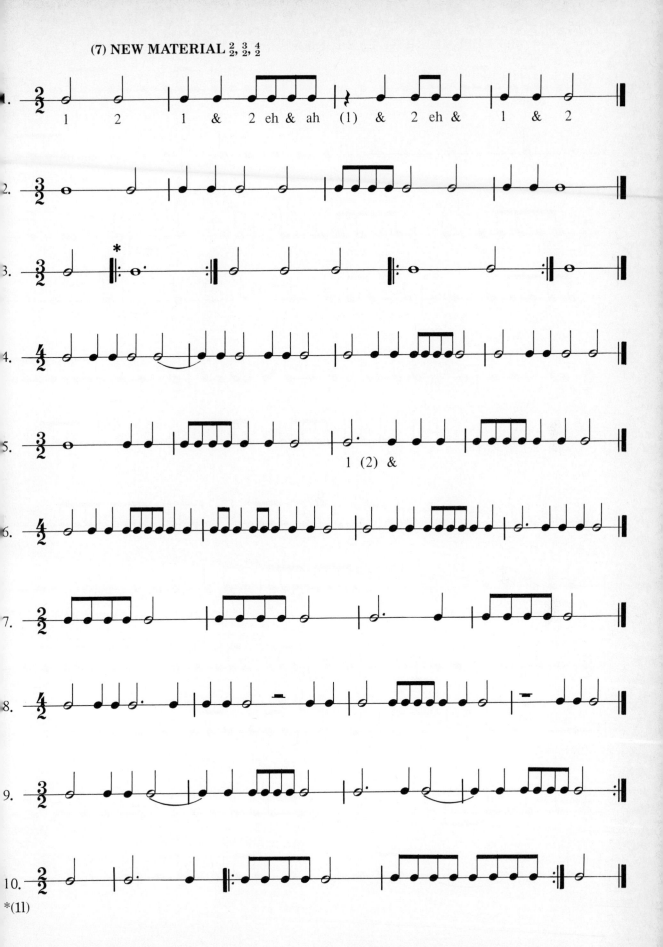

*(1l)

149

(8) EIGHT-MEASURE EXERCISES

1.   1   & ah   *Fine*

✶ *D.C. al Fine*

Fine

✶ *D.S. al Fine*

(11)

150

(9) NEW MATERIAL THE TRIPLET

In simple meters, count the triplet 1-eh-ah, 2-eh-ah. Once the triplet division of the beat (three equal notes) has been established, be sure you do not rush or speed up the subdivision (two equal notes) of the beat.

(10) EIGHT-MEASURE EXERCISES

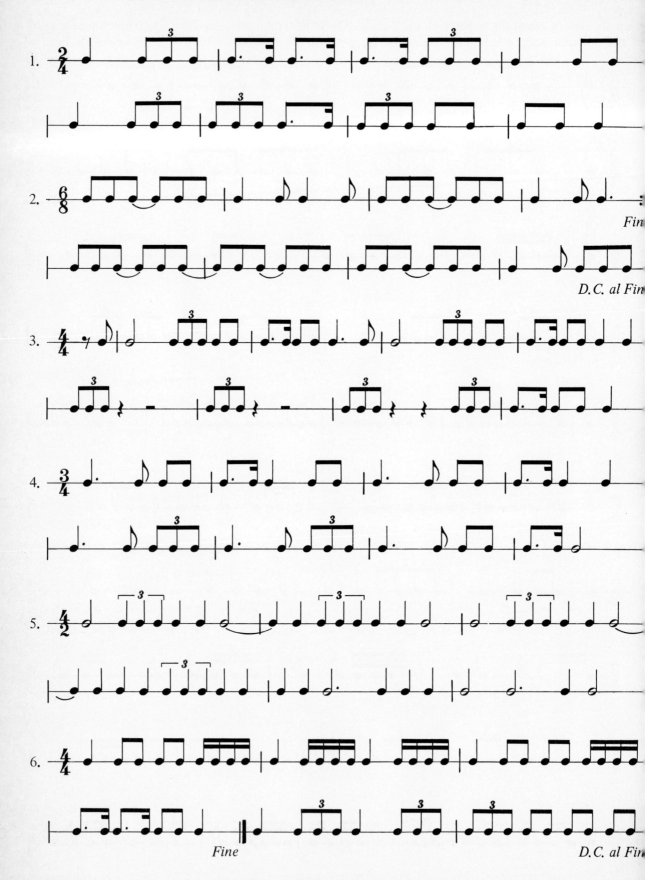

Fine

D.S. al Fine

Fine

D.C. al Fine

(11) COORDINATED-SKILL EXERCISES

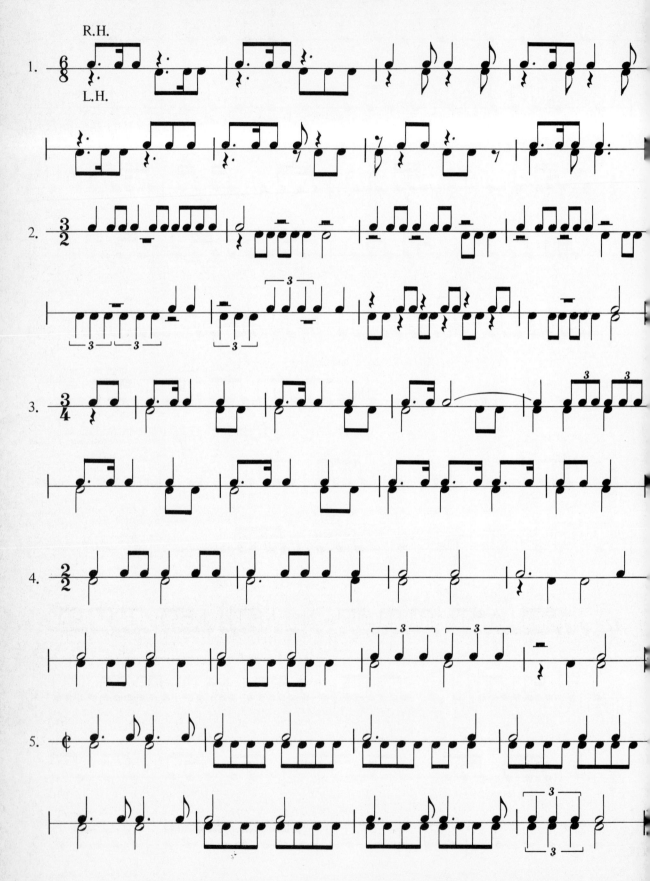

* *D.S. al coda*

(11)

155

(12) THREE-PART RHYTHMIC EXERCISES

1.

2.

Fin

D.C. al Fine

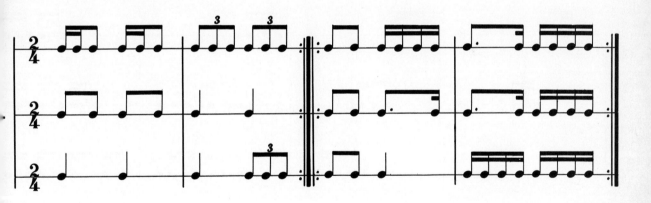

⨯ – with foot

5.

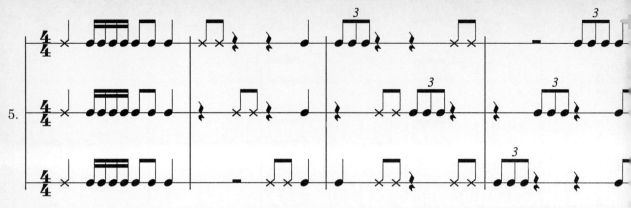

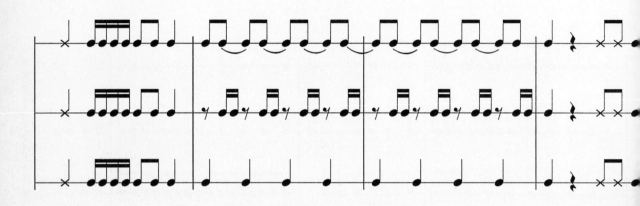

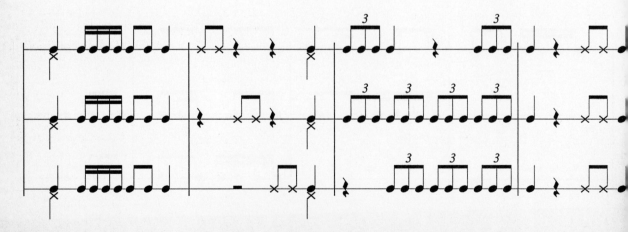

5b Solfeggio with Major Keys

Solfeggio (also called solfège or solmization) is a method of sight singing using the syllables *do-re-mi-fa-sol-la-ti(si)-do*. There are two systems. In the *fixed-do* system, *do* is C, regardless of the key. In the *movable-do* system, *do* moves according to the key. In the key of E♭, for example, E♭ is *do*; in the key of A, A is *do*. The movable-*do* system is best for the elementary student in the study of scales and intervals while in more advanced study, with the addition of frequent chromatics and key changes, the fixed-*do* system offers certain advantages. Both systems are included in the following examples.

The ability to sight-read music is a must for all music students. Not developing this skill will greatly inhibit your ability to learn and understand music literature, history, theory, and all other aspects of music. Solfeggio is an important method in the development of your sight-reading skill.

Sing the following examples by letter names, by numbers (see 2d), and by one of the two solmization methods. Note that *ti* is used in the movable-*do* system and is replaced by *si* in the fixed-*do* system. Also note these pronunciations:

> *do* is pronounced "doe"
> *fa* and *la* are pronounced "fah" and "lah"
> *re* is pronounced "ray"
> *mi*, *ti*, and *si* are pronounced "mee," "tee," and "see"

5c Melodic Exercises

(1) USING SOLFEGGIO SYLLABLES

159

*(6f)

ABA Form, Ternary Form, Song Form

The *D.C. al fine* creates an ABA (Ternary/Song) form. The opening "A" section is usually repeated. Th[e]
following "B" section is of contrasting material and in many cases in a different key. The D.C. returns yo[u]
to the beginning of Section "A" and concludes, without repeat, at the end of the "A" section, therefore a[n]
AABA form. This form was popular with classic and romantic composers and is the most common form fo[r]
our present day "pop" ballad.

(2) COORDINATED MELODIC-RHYTHMIC EXERCISES

Fine

D.C. al Fine

RHYTHMIC DICTATION

For longer rhythmic dictation examples combine any two or three exercises, of similar meter signature, into a single exercise.

MELODIC DICTATION

For longer melodic dictation examples combine two adjoining exercises into one.

(3) EIGHT-MEASURE EXERCISES

AB Form, Binary Form

The Binary form has two parts. The opening "A" section is repeated and the "B" section is usually repeated. The opening "A" and closing "B" sections may use similar or contrasting material. This form was popular in certain Baroque dance forms and in many early folk tunes. An example of Binary form is "The Star Spangled Banner."

(5) COORDINATED MELODIC-RHYTHMIC EXERCISES

RHYTHMIC DICTATION

For longer rhythmic dictation examples combine any two exercises, of similar meter signature, into a single exercise.

MELODIC DICTATION

For longer melodic dictation examples combine two adjoining exercises into one.

5d   Solfeggio with Minor Keys

The fixed-*do* system does not alter any syllable for chromatic alterations. In the movable-*do* system, the chromatic alterations of the diatonic major scale are as shown below. There is no chromatic tone between *mi* and *fa* or between *ti* and *do*; therefore, of course, no altered syllables are necessary.

do (di) re (ri) mi fa (fi) sol (si) la (li) ti do

do ti (te) la (le) sol (se) fa mi (me) re (rah) do

In the three minor forms, the syllables are altered as shown below.

A major do re mi fa sol la ti do   do re *me* fa sol *le* *te* do
a minor (natural)

do re *me* fa sol *le* ti do   do re *me* fa sol la ti do *te* *le* sol fa *me* re do
a minor (harmonic)   a minor (melodic)

(1) MELODIC EXERCISES

D Major

1.

d minor (melodic)

2.

sol   do   re me re   do   sol sol   le   sol la ti   do   do

le   me   me   le   me   la ti do

176

Roman numbers and arabic letters are uppercase for Major chords and lowercase for minor chords (6b). For the minor arabic letters a lowercase m or mi should be added.

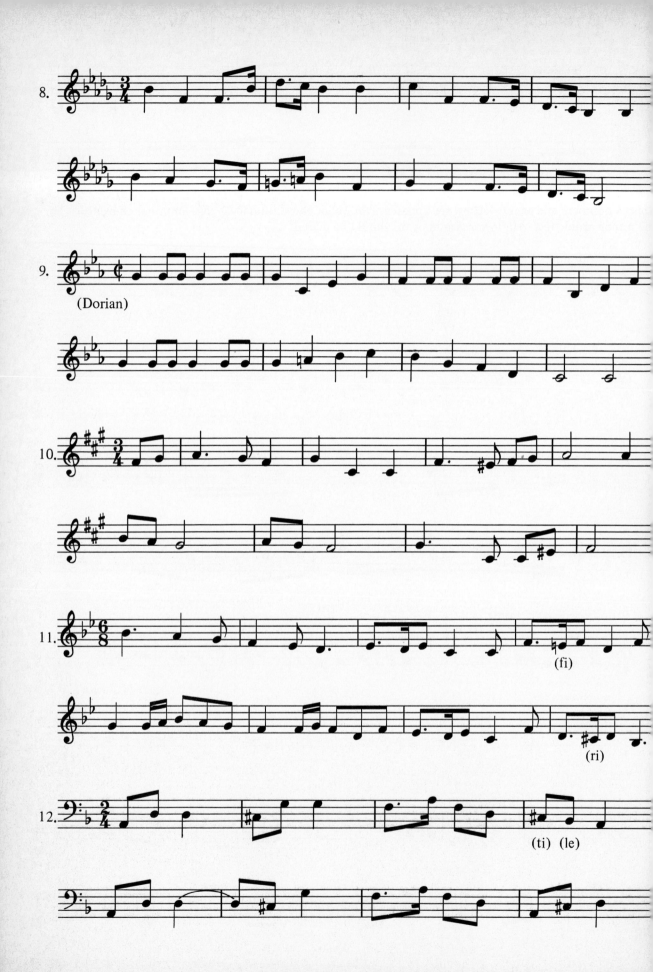

9. (Dorian)

11. (fi)

(ri)

12. (ti) (le)

7. FOUR PART ROUND (see pg. 81)

Charles Gounod

(2) COORDINATED MELODIC-RHYTHMIC EXERCISES

RHYTHMIC DICTATION

or longer rhythmic dictation examples combine any two exercises, of similar meter signature, into a ngle exercise.

MELODIC DICTATION

or longer melodic dictation examples combine two adjoining exercises into one.

A **chord** is several tones, generally three or more, played at the same time. The most common chord, the kind to be discussed in this unit, is constructed of consecutive intervals of the third. Chords can be, and are, constructed of intervals other than thirds, the most common being chords of consecutive intervals of the fourth. You may find it interesting to experiment in the construction and sounds of chords of the fourth.

6a   Triads

A **triad** is a three-tone chord combining a root and the intervals of a third and a fifth above the root. The *root* is the tone from which the chord is both constructed and named. All the chords in the following examples, therefore, are F chords in root position.

(1) MAJOR TRIADS

When the quality of the third is major and the quality of the fifth is perfect, the triad is **major**. A major triad may be constructed from any pitch by building these intervals above a given root. The major triad is the root, third, and fifth of any major scale.

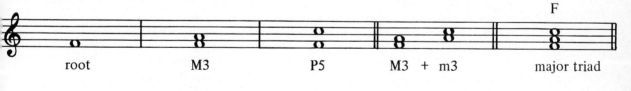

root   M3   P5   M3 + m3   major triad

(2) MINOR TRIADS

When the quality of the third is minor and the quality of the fifth is perfect, the triad is **minor**. A minor triad may be constructed from any pitch by building these intervals above a given root. The minor triad is the root, third, and fifth of any minor scale. It is a major triad with a lowered third.

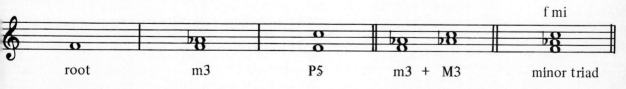

root   m3   P5   m3 + M3   minor triad

185

(3) DIMINISHED TRIADS

When the quality of the third is minor and the quality of the fifth is diminished, the triad is **diminished**
A diminished triad may be constructed from any pitch by building these intervals above a given root. It is a
major triad with a lowered third and fifth.

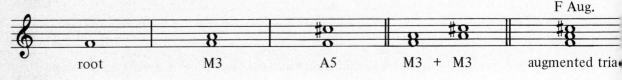

root   m3   d5   m3 + m3   diminished tria

(4) AUGMENTED TRIADS

When the quality of the third is major and the quality of the fifth is augmented, the triad is **augmented**
An augmented triad may be constructed from any pitch by building these intervals above a given root. It is
a major triad with a raised fifth.

root   M3   A5   M3 + M3   augmented tria

6b Chord Names and Symbols

Each scale step and its corresponding chord have a name that indicates their relationship to the tonic, the
name of the main tone of a key.

> tonic—the beginning pitch
> supertonic—the pitch *above* the tonic
> mediant—the pitch halfway between the tonic and the dominant
> subdominant—the dominant (five pitches) *below* the tonic
> dominant—the fifth pitch *above* the tonic
> submediant—the pitch a fifth *below* the mediant
> leading tone—half-step below the tonic; the pitch that "leads" back to the tonic
> or subtonic—whole-step below the tonic; the lowered seventh pitch in natural minor

Roman numerals are used to represent each chord constructed above the pitches of a scale. Capital
numerals are used for major chords, lowercase numerals for minor chords, lowercase numerals plus
small circle (∘) for diminished chords, and capital numerals plus a small plus sign (+) for augmented
chords.

Major scale degrees	Chord symbols	Chord names
1	I	tonic
2	ii	supertonic
3	iii	mediant
4	IV	subdominant
5	V	dominant
6	vi	submediant
7	vii°	"leading tone"

The triads built above the C major scale and their corresponding numbers are shown in the following
example.

6c

Root-Position Triad Table

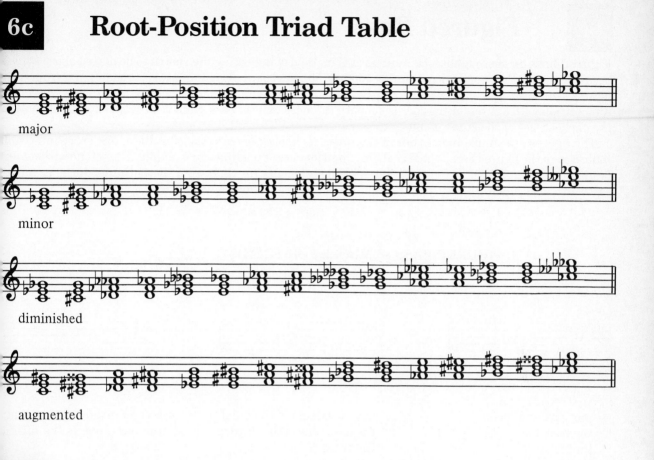

major

minor

diminished

augmented

6d

Root Position and Inversion

When the root of a triad is in the bass—that is, when the root is the lowest tone sounded—the chord is in root position. If any other tone is in the bass, the chord is **inverted**. If the third of the triad is in the bass, the chord is in first inversion; if the fifth is in the bass, the chord is in second inversion.

Root-position and inverted C major chords are shown below in two positions—*close position*, in which all the notes are within one octave, and *open position*, in which the notes span more than an octave.

Root position—C, on which the C major chord is built, is the lowest tone sounded.

close position   open position

First inversion—The third of the chord is the lowest tone sounded.

close position   open position

Second inversion—The fifth of the chord is the lowest tone sounded.

close position   open position

Figured Bass

Figured bass (or thoroughbass) is a numerical method of indicating the chords to be played above a given bass line. In the Baroque period (roughly 1600–1750), keyboard players improvised their parts from these figures—that is, their part was not written out in their score; it consisted only of the bass line of the composition with figures for the chords beneath it. These figured-bass symbols are still extensively used in the early stages of the study of music theory.

The figures are simple indications of the *intervals above the bass tone* of a chord. Not every interval is indicated in the figured bass, which is abbreviated for ease of reading. For example, a bass tone without any figures indicates a triad in root position, and the other figures that are in parentheses in the example below are also generally omitted. Chromatic alterations are indicated by the symbols shown.

(1) FIGURED-BASS SYMBOLS FOR TRIADS

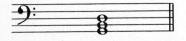
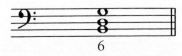

(5) root-position triad;
(3) the bass tone is the root of the triad

6 first inversion of the triad;
(3) the bass tone is the third of the triad

6 second inversion of a triad;
4 the bass tone is the fifth of the triad

(2) REALIZATION

Translating the arabic numbers into the correct notes above the given bass line is simple, but in performance practice can be very difficult. In "realization" the performer uses the figure bass only as an outline for a more complex "improvised" accompaniment that compliments the overall musical work.

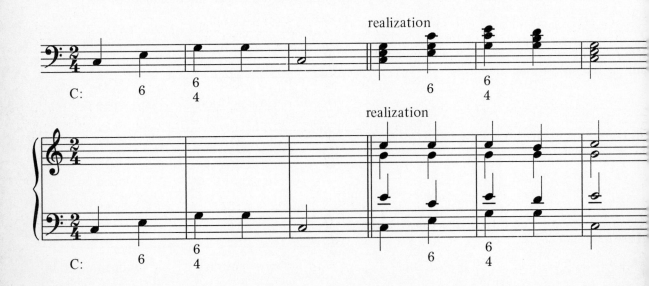

6f Primary Triads

The three most important triads are the **primary triads**—those constructed above the first, fourth, and fifth pitches of the major or minor scale. Those constructed above the second, third, sixth, and seventh pitches are called *secondary chords*. They are the three major triads in the diatonic major scale, and they have a particularly close harmonic relationship: the dominant (V) lies a perfect fifth above the tonic, and the subdominant (IV) lies a perfect fifth below the tonic.

The tonic triad (I), constructed on the first scale degree, ranks first in importance. Tonal musical compositions (music with a clearly defined key) often begin and almost invariably end on the tonic chord.

The dominant triad exercises great harmonic influence, especially with the addition of a seventh (see 6f). The dominant chord is second in importance, and the subdominant is third.

Below is a list of the primary triads of all the major scales. Play these triads on the piano until your hand and ear are thoroughly familiar with them.

In the *natural* minor form, all of the primary triads are minor (i-iv-v). This is the least used of the minor forms. In the *harmonic* minor form, the tonic and subdominant are minor and the dominant is major (i-iv-V). In the ascending *melodic* minor form, the tonic is minor and the subdominant and dominant are major (i-IV-V). In the descending *melodic* minor form, all of the primary triads are minor (the *natural* minor form i-iv-v).

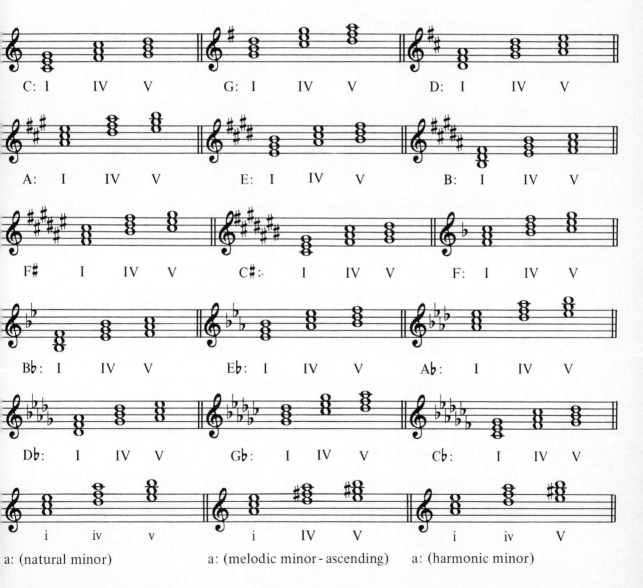

189

6g Seventh Chords

A four-tone chord combining a triad and the interval of a seventh above the root is called a **seventh chord**. Like all chords, seventh chords can be constructed on any given pitch.

(1) MAJOR-MINOR SEVENTH CHORDS

When the quality of the triad is major and the quality of the seventh is minor, the chord is called a **major-minor seventh chord**. Of all the seventh chords, it is the most frequently used.

This chord is called the **dominant seventh chord** when it is built above the *fifth* scale degree. As we have seen, the dominant triad (V) is second in importance only to the tonic triad; similarly, the dominant seventh is harmonically a very important chord.

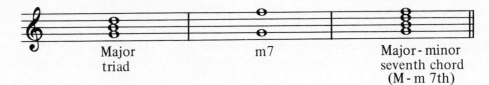

(2) MAJOR SEVENTH CHORDS

When the quality of the triad is major and the quality of the seventh is major, the chord is called a **major seventh chord**.

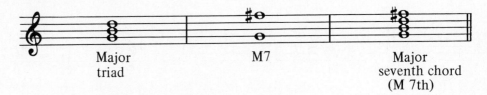

(3) MINOR SEVENTH CHORDS

When the quality of the triad is minor and the quality of the seventh is minor, the chord is called a **minor seventh chord**.

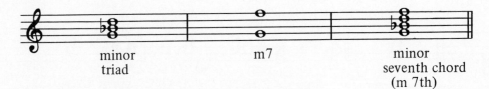

(4) HALF-DIMINISHED SEVENTH CHORDS

When the quality of the triad is diminished and the quality of the seventh is minor, the chord is called a **half-diminished seventh chord**. The half-diminished seventh chord can also be considered a minor seventh chord with its fifth pitch lowered—therefore, a minor seventh, flat five.

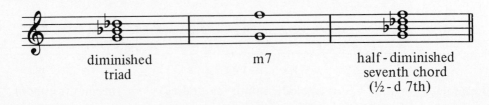

(5) DIMINISHED SEVENTH CHORDS

When the quality of the triad is diminished and the quality of the seventh is diminished, the chord is called **diminished seventh chord**.

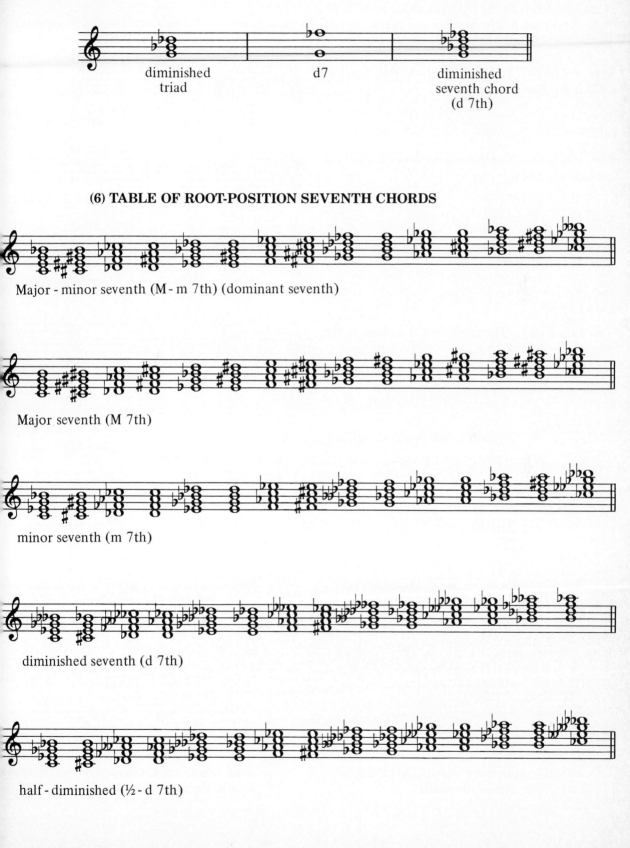

diminished
triad

d7

diminished
seventh chord
(d 7th)

(6) TABLE OF ROOT-POSITION SEVENTH CHORDS

Major - minor seventh (M - m 7th) (dominant seventh)

Major seventh (M 7th)

minor seventh (m 7th)

diminished seventh (d 7th)

half - diminished (½ - d 7th)

(7) SEVENTH-CHORD INVERSIONS

When the root of a seventh chord is in the bass—that is, when it is the lowest tone sounded—the seventh chord is in root position. If any other tone is in the bass, the chord is inverted. If the third of the seventh chord is in the bass, the chord is in first inversion. If the fifth is in the bass, the chord is in second inversion. If the seventh is in the bass, the chord is in third inversion.

Root-position and inverted major-minor seventh chords are shown below in both close and open position.

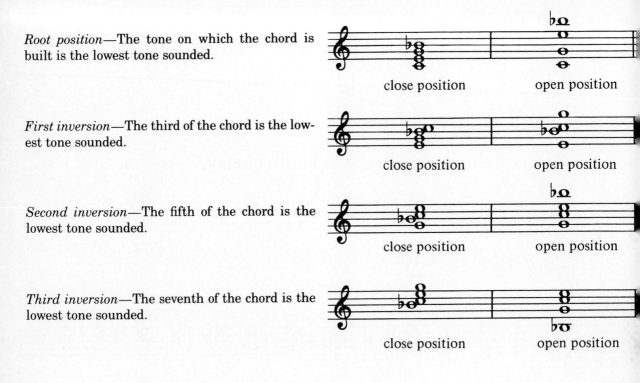

Root position—The tone on which the chord is built is the lowest tone sounded.

close position   open position

First inversion—The third of the chord is the lowest tone sounded.

close position   open position

Second inversion—The fifth of the chord is the lowest tone sounded.

close position   open position

Third inversion—The seventh of the chord is the lowest tone sounded.

close position   open position

(8) FIGURED-BASS SYMBOLS FOR SEVENTH CHORDS

7
(5) root-position seventh chord; the bass tone is
3   the root of the chord

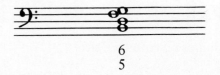

6
5   first inversion of a seventh chord; the bass
(3) tone is the third of the chord

(6) second inversion of a seventh chord; the bass
4   tone is the fifth of the chord
(3)

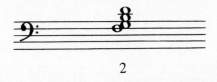

(6) third inversion of a seventh chord; the bass
(4) tone is the seventh of the chord
2

(9) CHROMATIC ALTERATIONS

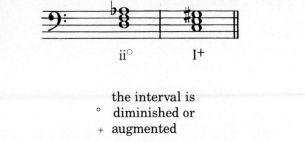

ii°   I+

the interval is
° diminished or
+ augmented

a diagonal line through
a number raises the tone
one half step

\#   ♭   ♮

when used *alone*, these accidentals affect the
third of a root-position triad

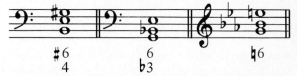

\#6   6   ♮6
4   ♭3

\#   when *preceding a number*, these accidentals
♭   indicate a corresponding alteration of the tone
♮   represented by that number

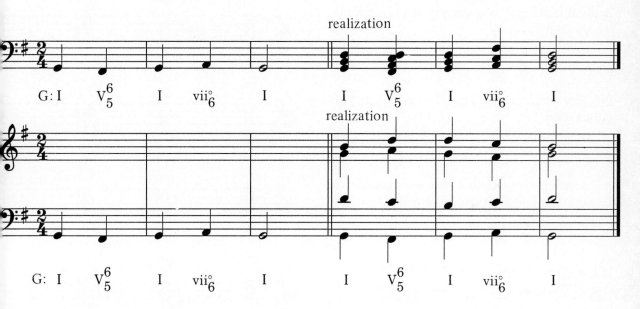

realization

G: I   V$^6_5$ I   vii°$_6$ I   I   V$^6_5$ I   vii°$_6$ I

realization

G: I   V$^6_5$ I   vii°$_6$ I   I   V$^6_5$ I   vii°$_6$ I

In the study of music theory the figured-bass is used to indicate if a chord is root position or an inversion. In commercial music letters are placed above the staff to indicate the desired chord. Inversions of the chord are indicated by first the chord letter, a slash mark, and then the desired *root note* (bass note) placed below. C over E would be a first inversion, C over G a second inversion.

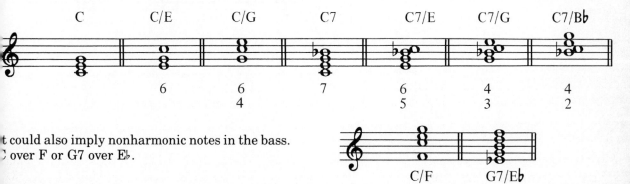

C   C/E   C/G   C7   C7/E   C7/G   C7/B♭

6   6   7   6   4   4
         4   5   3   2

It could also imply nonharmonic notes in the bass.
C over F or G7 over E♭.

C/F   G7/E♭

6h   Commercial Chord Symbols

The chord symbols used in commercial music are different from those used in theory classes. The symbols are not completely uniform in all printed commercial music, but the principles are standard. Symbols are always placed above the staff. (For simplicity, all the examples below are notated in C.)

A capital letter stands for a major triad. When the root is flat or sharp, the flat or sharp is added to the letter name even if it is in the key signature.

Minor, augmented, and diminished triads, respectively, are indicated by adding one of the following to the letter name: *m*, *min*, or *mi*; + or *aug*; ° or *dim*.

A diminished symbol normally implies a diminished seventh.

A 6 adds a major sixth above the root of a major or minor triad.

A 7 adds a minor seventh. The minor seventh can be added to major, minor, diminished, and augmented triads.

Major sevenths are usually added only to major triads. The symbol for this chord is M7, maj7, or 7.

A 9 signifies a ninth chord. The basic structure is a major-minor (dominant) seventh chord plus a major ninth.

TABLE OF COMMERCIAL CHORD SYMBOLS

SYMBOLS FOR TRIADS

Symbol	Triad	Interval added above root
7th or 7	major	minor 7th
6th or 6	major	major 6th
m7	minor	minor 7th
m6	minor	major 6th
M7, Ma, Maj, or 7̶	major	major 7th
dim or 7°	diminished	diminished 7th
7 (+5) or aug.	augmented	minor 7th
m7 (♭5)	diminished	minor 7th
7 (♭5)	major with dim. 5th	minor 7th

SYMBOLS FOR OTHER CHORDS

Symbol	Chord	Interval added above root
9th or 9	7th	major 9th
7 (♭9)	7th	minor 9th
+11 or aug. 11	7th, 9th (or 13th)	augmented 11th (compound aug. 4th)
13	7th	13th (compound major 6th)
+9 or aug. 9	7th	aug. 9th (enharmonic minor 10th)
m9	m7th	major 9th
m11	m7th or 9th	perfect 11th

Construct the indicated triads *above* the following notes. Please note that a majority of diminished triads above *flat notes* will require double flats (♭♭). Augmented chords above a *sharp note* will require a double sharp (×).

In writing the required accidentals above a given note the accidentals should be staggered from right to left to right and should not be written in a straight vertical line.

Correct   Incorrect

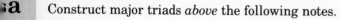

Construct major triads *above* the following notes.

Construct minor triads *above* the following notes.

Construct diminished triads *above* the following notes.

Construct augmented triads *above* the following notes.

Worksheet 6-3

Construct the following triad chords using the given note as the *root* of the chord.

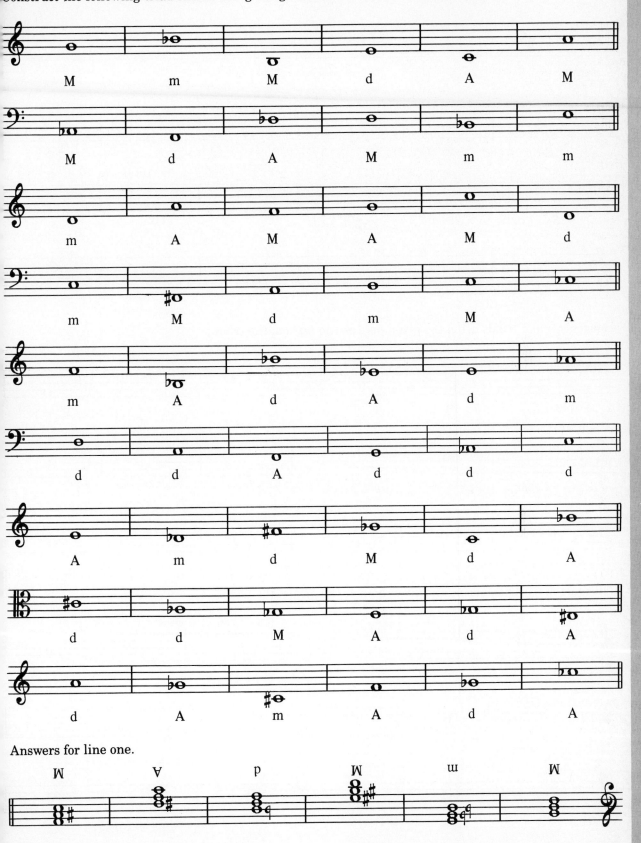

Answers for line one.

6a
(1)

Construct major triads using the given note as the *root* of the triad.

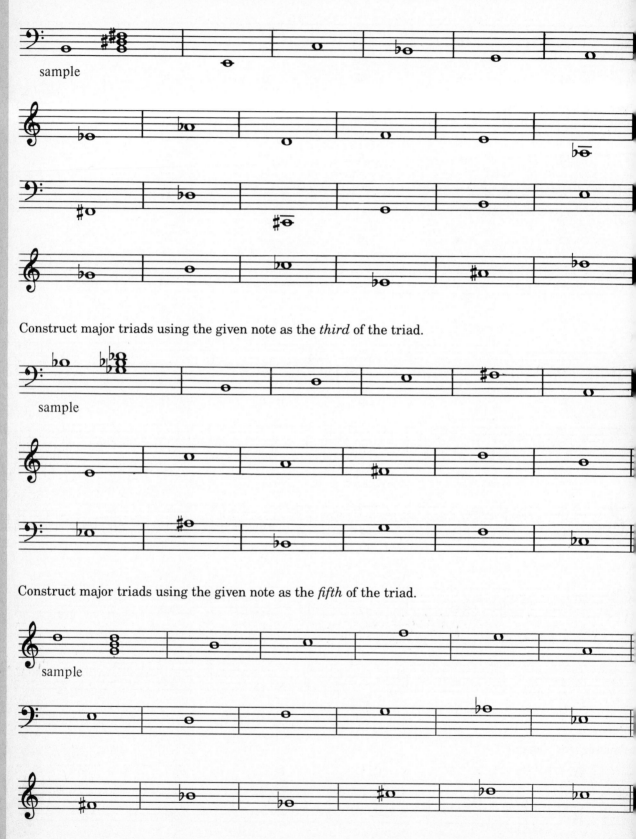

sample

Construct major triads using the given note as the *third* of the triad.

sample

Construct major triads using the given note as the *fifth* of the triad.

sample

Construct minor and diminished triads using the given note as the *root* of the triad.

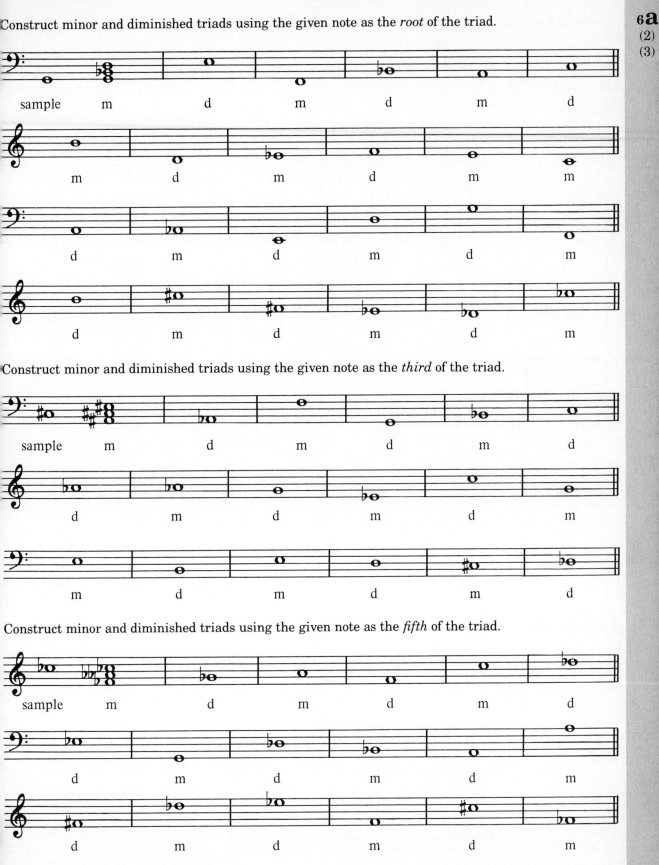

Construct minor and diminished triads using the given note as the *third* of the triad.

Construct minor and diminished triads using the given note as the *fifth* of the triad.

Worksheet 6-6

Construct augmented triads using the given note as the *root* of the triad.

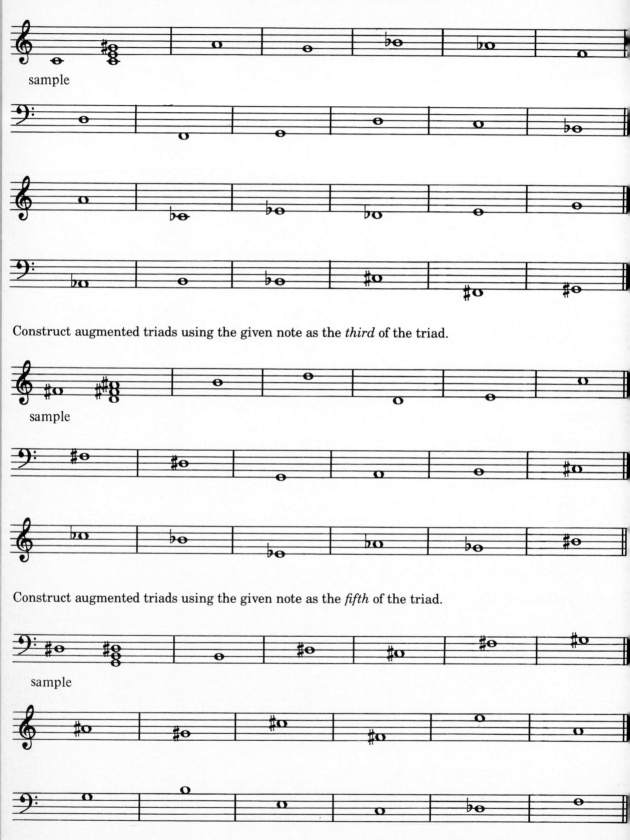

sample

Construct augmented triads using the given note as the *third* of the triad.

sample

Construct augmented triads using the given note as the *fifth* of the triad.

sample

202

Identify the following triads.

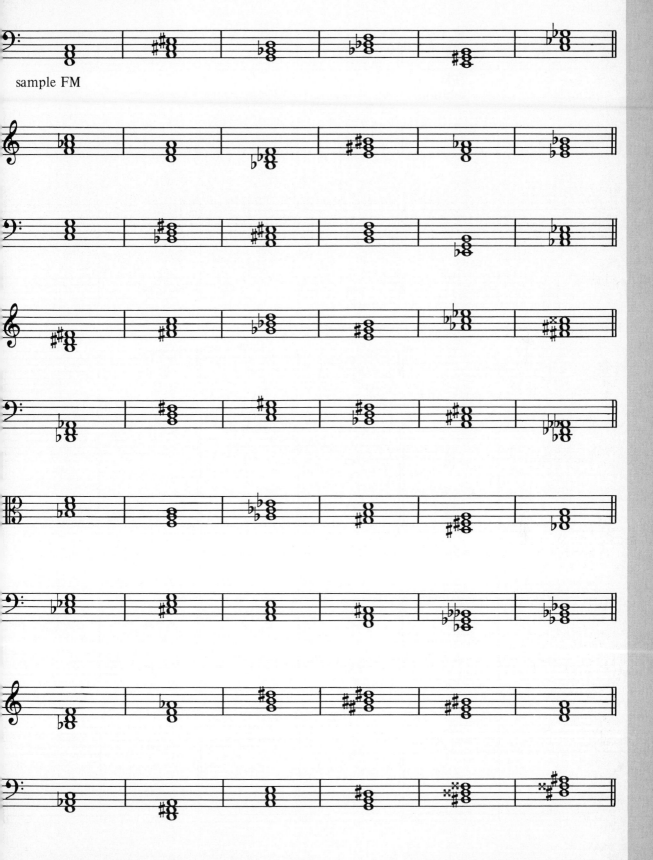

sample FM

6c
6d

Reduce each of the following chords to a single closed root-position triad. Identify each chord by name an quality.

sample　　　　　　　　FM
　　　　　　　　　　solution

sample　　　　　　solution

Write the three major triads—tonic (I), subdominant (IV), and dominant (V)—in each of the following major keys. Label each with the key and the proper roman numerals.

6f

F: I   IV   V
sample

Write the three minor triads and the one diminished triad—supertonic (ii), mediant (iii), submediant (vi), and leading tone (vii°)—in each of the following major keys. Label each with the key and the proper roman numerals.

6b

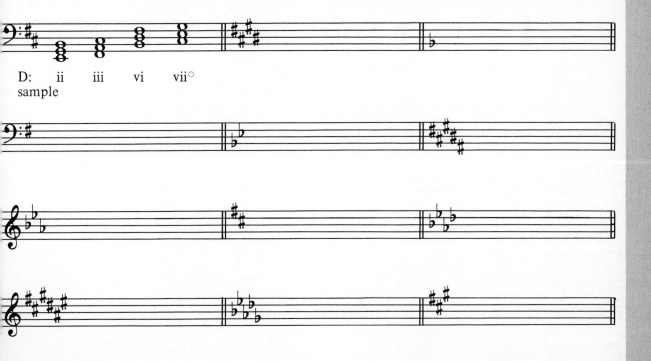

D: ii   iii   vi   vii°
sample

     205

6b Write the three minor triads—tonic (i), subdominant (iv), and dominant (v)—in each of the followin[g] minor keys. Label each with the key and the proper roman numerals.

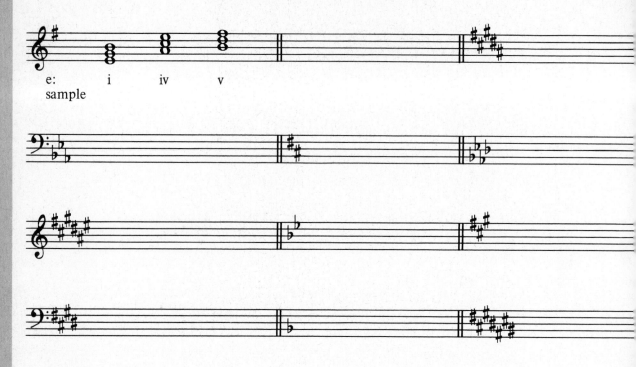

e: i   iv   v
sample

Write the three major triads and the one diminished triad—supertonic (ii°), mediant (III) submediant (VI[)] and subtonic (VII)—in each of the following minor keys. Label each with the key and the proper roma[n] numerals.

a: ii°   III   VI   VII
sample

Construct appropriate chords above the following figured-bass symbols. Label the chords to indicate their root-position name and quality.

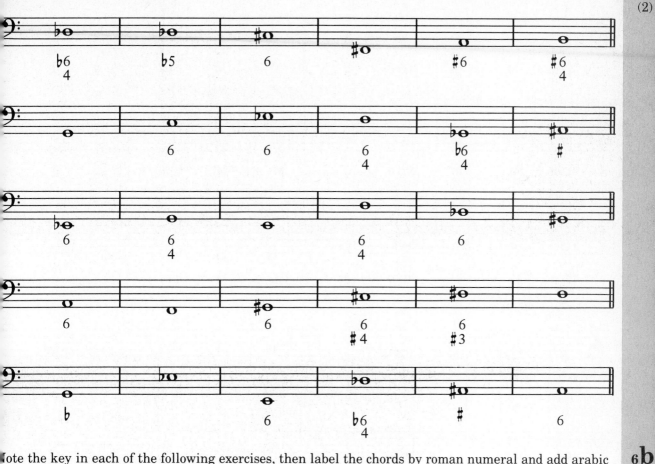

Note the key in each of the following exercises, then label the chords by roman numeral and add arabic numbers to indicate the inversion. Be sure to review "figured bass" (6e).

6g Construct the following seventh chords using the given note as the *root* of the chord.

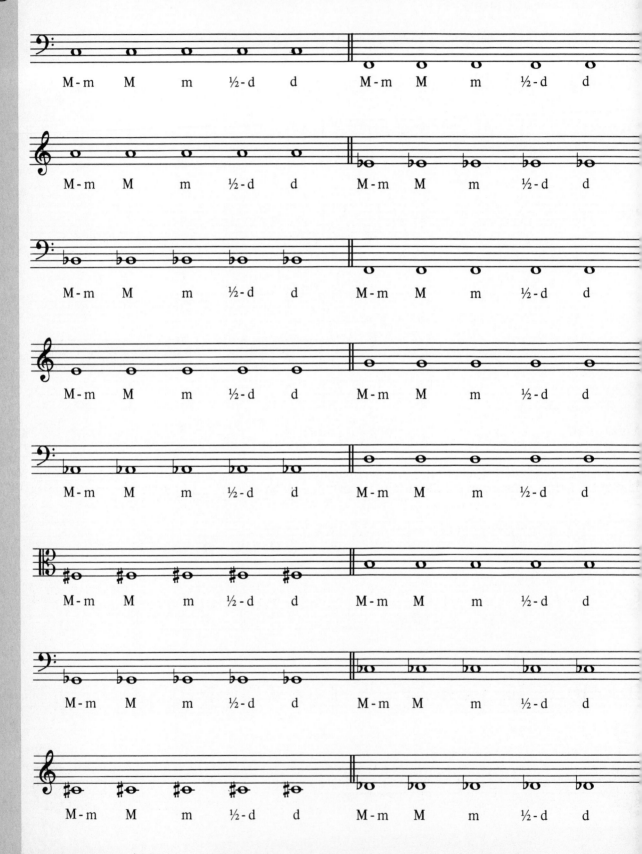

NAME _____

Construct major-minor seventh chords above the following notes.

Construct major seventh chords above the following notes.

Worksheet 6-14

Construct minor seventh chords above the following notes.

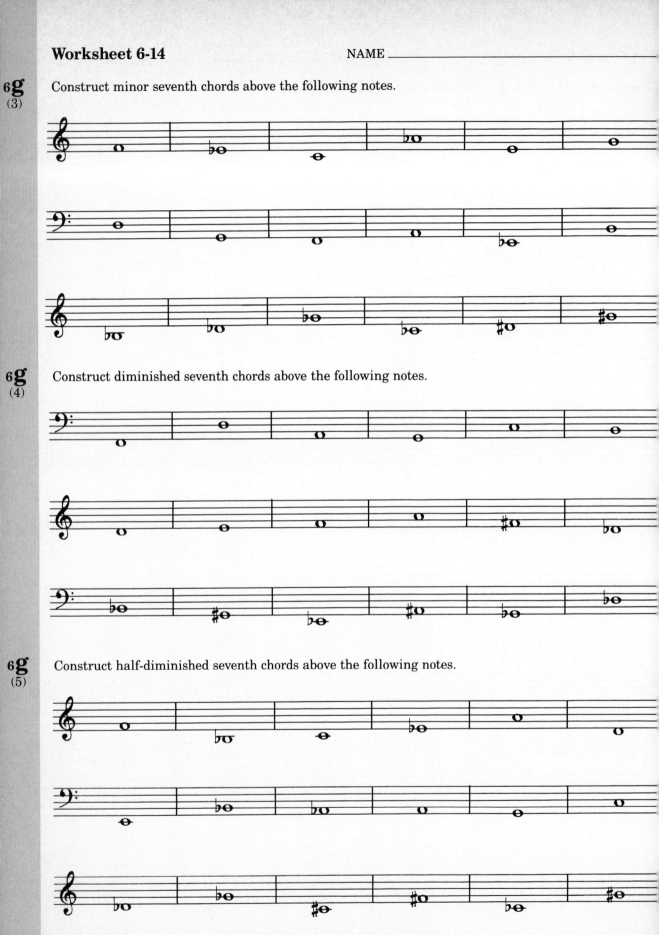

Construct diminished seventh chords above the following notes.

Construct half-diminished seventh chords above the following notes.

Worksheet 6-15

NAME _____

Construct the following seventh chords using the given note as the *root* of the chord.

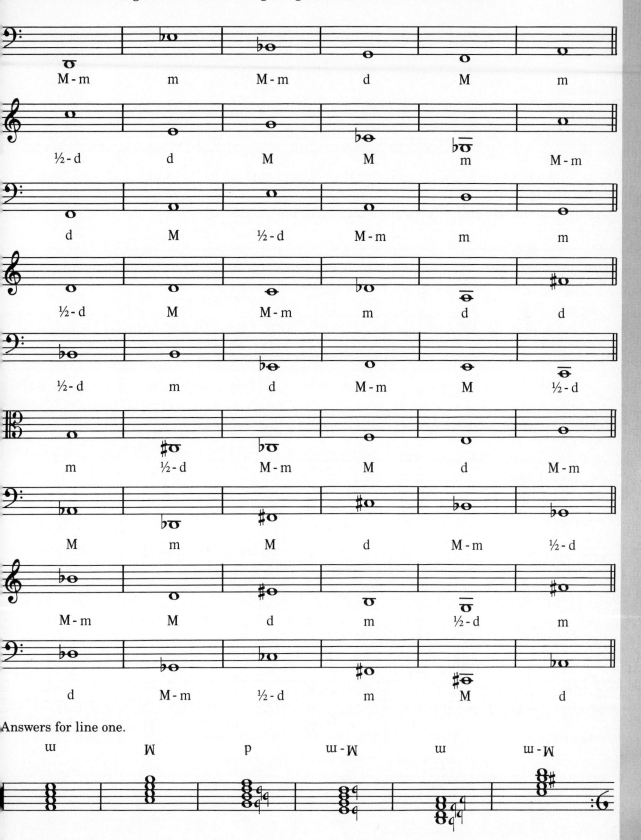

Answers for line one.

6g Construct the following seventh chords using the given note as the *root* of the chord.

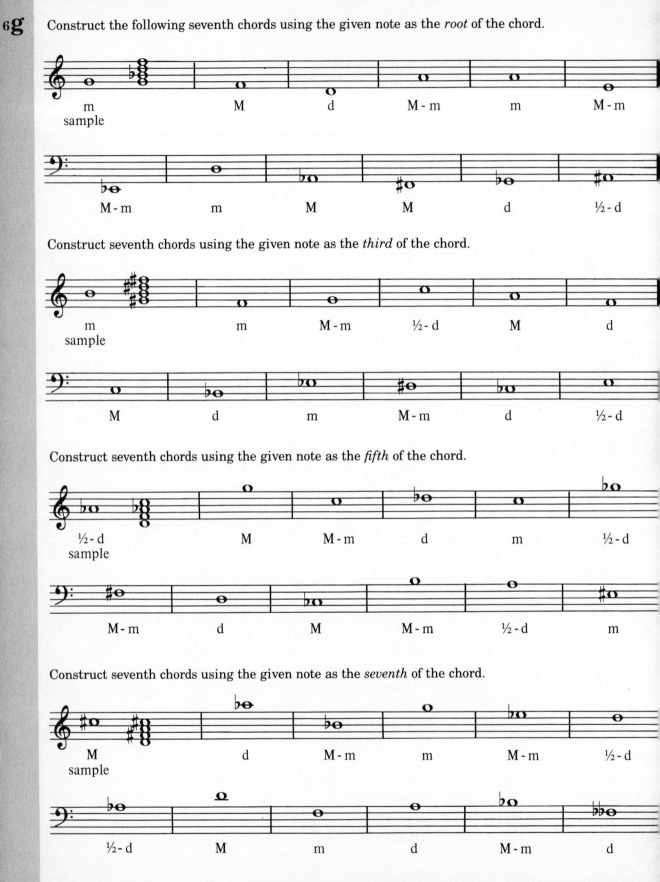

Construct seventh chords using the given note as the *third* of the chord.

Construct seventh chords using the given note as the *fifth* of the chord.

Construct seventh chords using the given note as the *seventh* of the chord.

Worksheet 6-17

NAME _____

Identify the following seventh chords.

NAME _____

Reduce each of the following seventh chords to single close root-position chords. Identify chord by name and quality.

d min 7

sample   solution

sample   solution

NAME _____

Construct the primary chords—I-IV-V7—for the following major and minor keys.

6f

d: (har.)   a: (nat.)   F#:

eb: (nat.)   G: Gb:

g#:(mel.)   Db: c#:(har.)

Ab: C: D:

A: g: (har.)   c: (mel.)

Eb: f#:(har.)   C#:

b: (nat.)   E: Cb:

c: (mel.)   Bb: ab: (har.)

F: B: e: (mel.)

6e
(2)
(3)

Construct appropriate chords above the following figured-bass symbols. Label the chords to indicate the root-position name and quality.

sample 6/4   GM   7   6   7/#   #7♭7   4/3

6/5   #4/3   7   4/2   7/#   #6/5

4/2   4/3   7/♭5   6/5   ♭4/3   4/♭2

6/5/#3   7/#5   4/3   ♭7/♭5/♭3   6/5   6/5/#3

♭6/4/♭3   ♭6/♭5   7/#5   7   #6/4/3   4/2

6b

6e
(2)
(3)

Note the key in each of the following exercises, then label the chords by roman numeral and add arabi numbers to indicate the inversion.

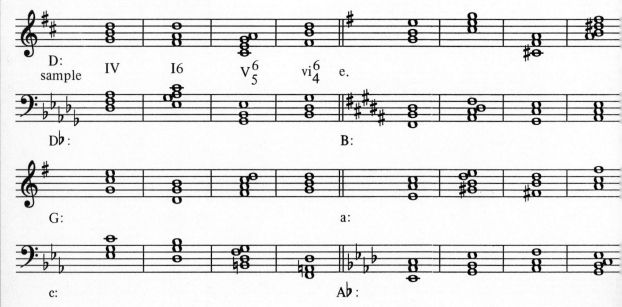

D:
sample   IV   I6   V⁶₅   vi⁶₄   e.

D♭ :   B:

G: a:

c: A♭ :

1. Construct the indicated triads using the given note as the *root* of the triad.

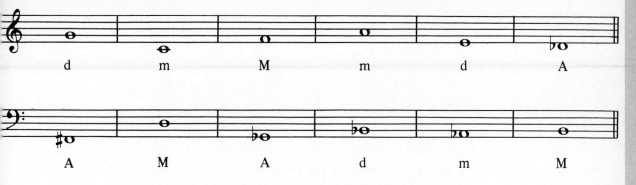

2. Construct the indicated triads using the given note as the third of the triad.

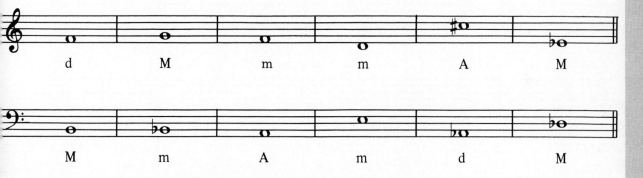

3. Construct the indicated triads using the given note as the fifth of the triad.

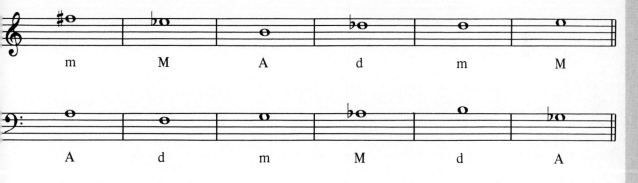

4. Identify the following triads.

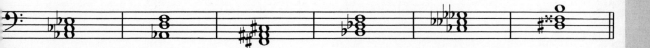

5. Construct the primary chords—I-IV-V7—for the following major and minor keys.

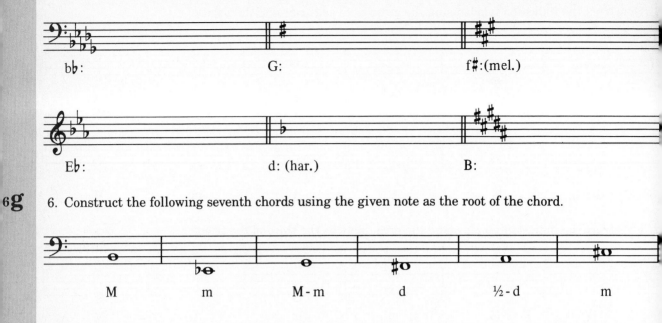

bb: G: f#:(mel.)

Eb: d: (har.)   B:

6. Construct the following seventh chords using the given note as the root of the chord.

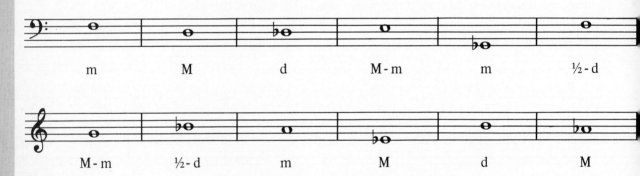

M   m   M-m   d   ½-d   m

d   M-m   ½-d   M   m   d

7. Construct seventh chords using the given note as the third of the chord.

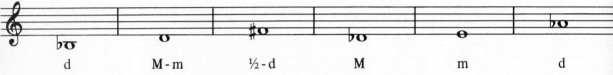

m   M   d   M-m   m   ½-d

M-m   ½-d   m   M   d   M

8. Construct seventh chords using the given note as the fifth of the chord.

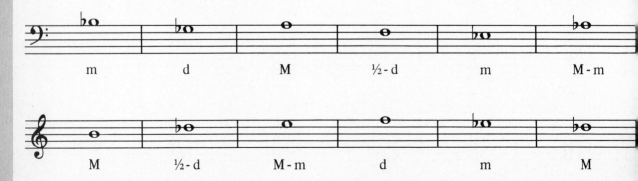

m   d   M   ½-d   m   M-m

M   ½-d   M-m   d   m   M

9. Construct seventh chords using the given note as the seventh of the chord.

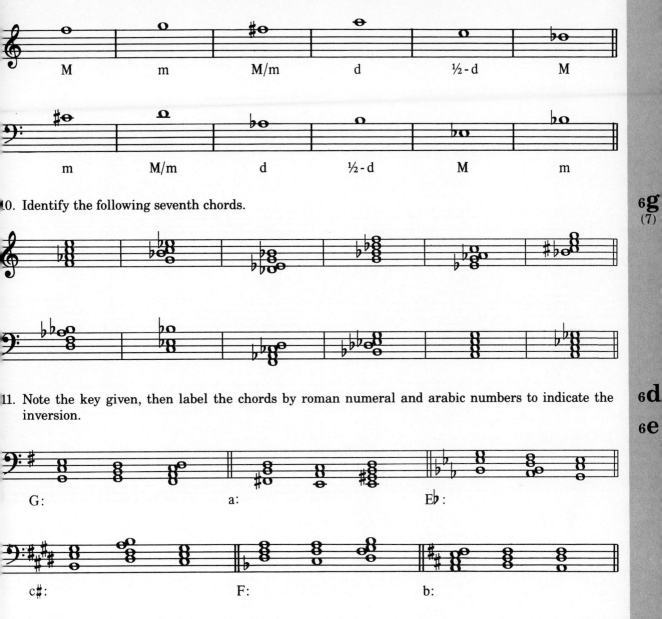

M   m   M/m   d   ½-d   M

m   M/m   d   ½-d   M   m

10. Identify the following seventh chords.

11. Note the key given, then label the chords by roman numeral and arabic numbers to indicate the inversion.

G: a: Eb:

c#:   F: b:

12. Construct appropriate chords above the following figured-bass symbols. Label the chords and indicate their root-position name and quality.

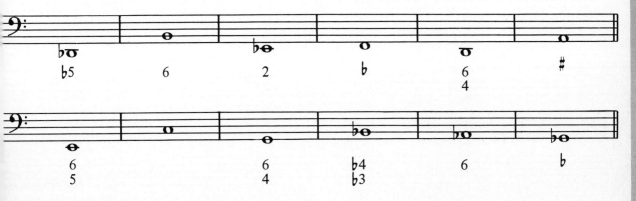

b5   6   2   b   6   #
                                        4

6   o   6   b4   6   b
5   4   b3

Rhythmic and Melodic Exercises—Difficult

7a Mixed Rhythmic Units

Any note may be subdivided into any number of notes. A quarter note, for example, regularly divides into two and subdivides into four, eight, and sixteen. But a quarter note may also be subdivided into three, five, six, seven, nine, etc. The desired number of notes is beamed or bracketed, with a number placed above the beam or bracket to indicate the number of notes in the group.

In simple meters, the total durational value of the triplet (division into three) is always the same as the value of the duplet (division into two). For example, the three eighths of a quarter-note triplet have the same total value as the two eighths of the normal division. If the number of subdivided notes exceeds twice the number in a regular division, the irregular group uses the next smaller note value. Thus, a quarter note subdivides into four, five, six, or seven sixteenth notes; for eight or more subdivisions, into 32nd notes; and for sixteen or more subdivisions, into 64th notes.

etc.

The following examples show the same rhythmic pattern in three simple duple meters.

In compound meters, the total durational value of the duplet (two) is always the same as the value of the triplet (the first division in compound meters). For example, the two eighths of a dotted-quarter-note duplet have the same value as the three eighths of the normal division. If the number of subdivided notes exceeds twice the number in a regular division, the same rule applies as in the simple duple meter. That is, a dotted quarter note subdivides into two, three, four, or five eighth notes; for six or more subdivisions, into sixteenth notes; and for twelve or more subdivisions, into 32nd notes.

etc.

The following examples show the same rhythmic pattern in three simple triple meters.

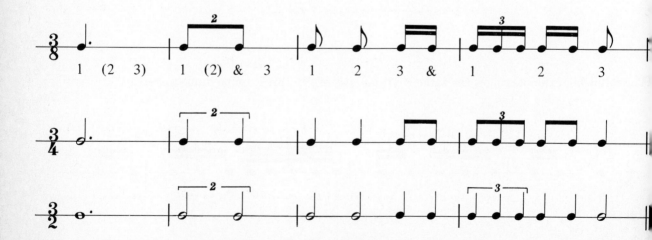

(1) SIMPLE AND COMPOUND METERS

(2) EIGHT-MEASURE RHYTHMIC EXERCISES

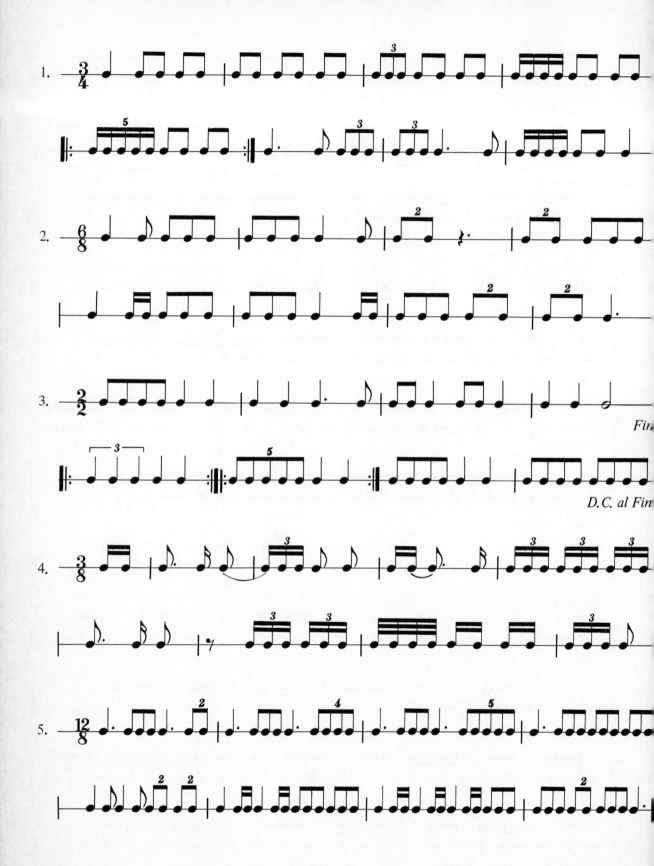

Fir[...]

D.C. al Fin[...]

(3) COORDINATED-SKILL EXERCISES

7b Mixed Meters—Constant Note Values

A form of rhythmic and metric embellishment occurs when two different meter signatures are used in the same work. Changing meter signatures during a work serves to shift the location of the strong beat. In the following examples of mixed meters, the *note value* of the beat remains constant.

(1) EIGHT-MEASURE RHYTHMIC EXERCISES

(2) COORDINATED-SKILL EXERCISES

7c Mixed Meters—Changing Note Values

If simple and compound meter signatures are combined, the composer may indicate the relationship between note values above the staff. In the first example below, for instance, the notes above the staff indicate that the dotted quarter note in measure 2 equals the preceding quarter note, and that the quarter note in measure 3 equals the preceding dotted quarter note.

(1) EIGHT-MEASURE RHYTHMIC EXERCISES

Fin

D.C. al Fin

7d Syncopation

Syncopation is, generally speaking, a deliberate displacement of the normal pulse or beat of the meter. Our sense of rhythm depends on the recurrence of groups of two or three equal beats each, with an accent on the first beat of each group. Any shifting of the accent to the normally weak beat(s) of the measure is syncopation. The following examples show the same syncopated rhythmic pattern in three simple duple meters.

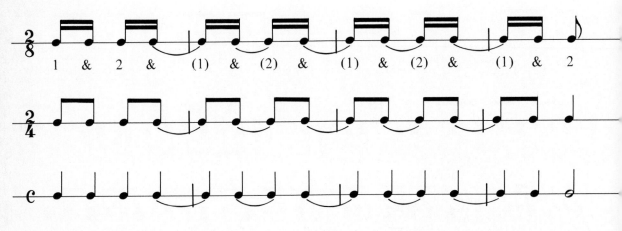

The following examples show the same syncopated rhythmic pattern in three simple triple meters.

233

(1) EIGHT-MEASURE RHYTHMIC EXERCISES

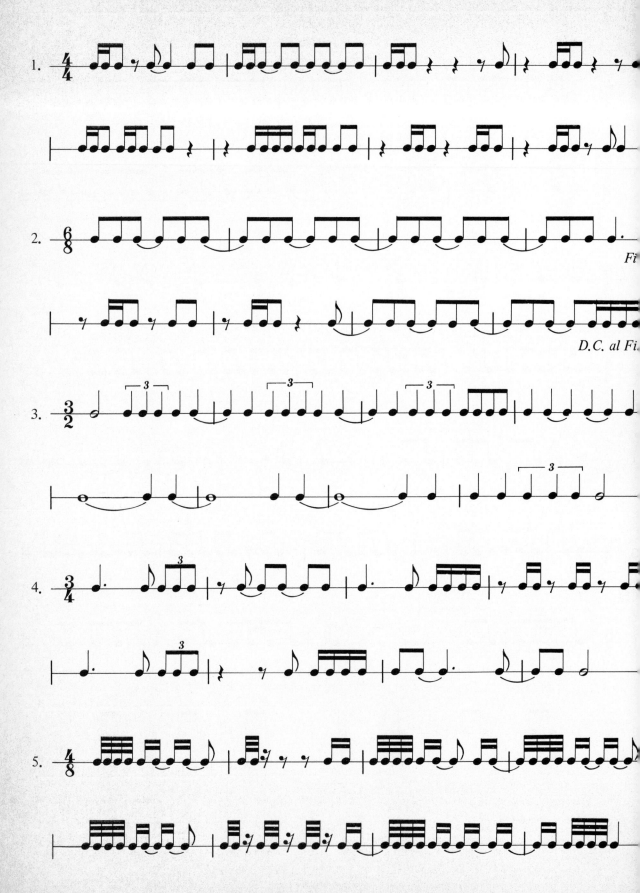

Fi

D.C. al Fi.

(2) COORDINATED-SKILL EXERCISES

(3) THREE-PART RHYTHMIC EXERCISES

These exercises are for group participation, with at least one person on each line. Divide the parts among the performers, establish a beat, and begin. Perform each exercise a second and third time, with the performers tapping a different part each time.

A real test of your coordinated skills is to practice the exercises by yourself, tapping the bottom line with your foot, the middle line with your left hand, and the top line with your right hand.

*See page 282.

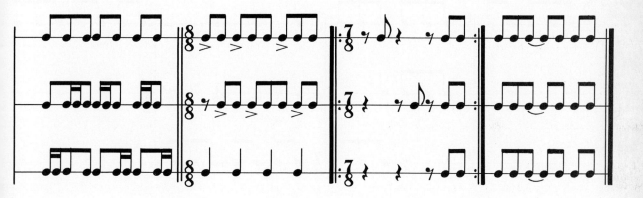

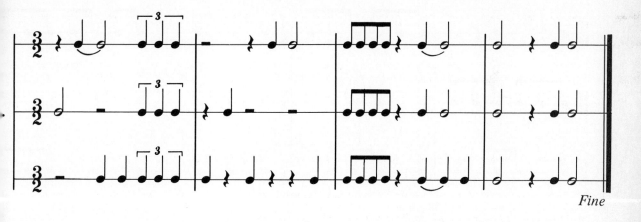

Fine

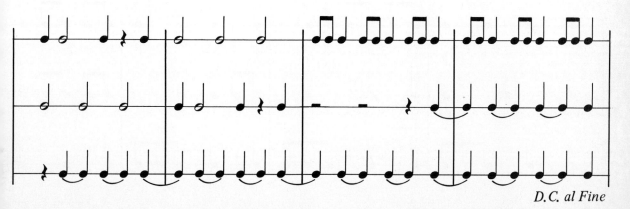

D.C. al Fine

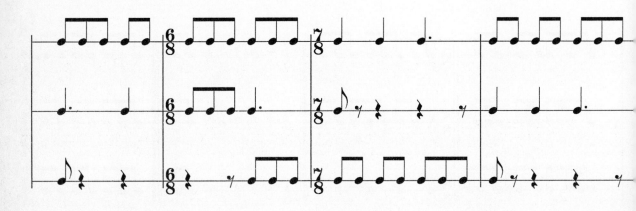

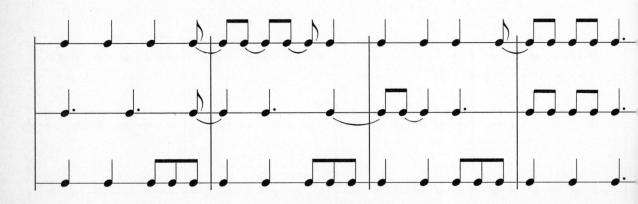

Melodic Exercises

(1) MIXED RHYTHMIC UNITS

(1b3)

6.

7.

8.

9.

10. soprano clef*

* (1b 3)

(2) COORDINATED MELODIC-RHYTHMIC EXERCISES

(3) MIXED METERS—CONSTANT NOTE VALUES

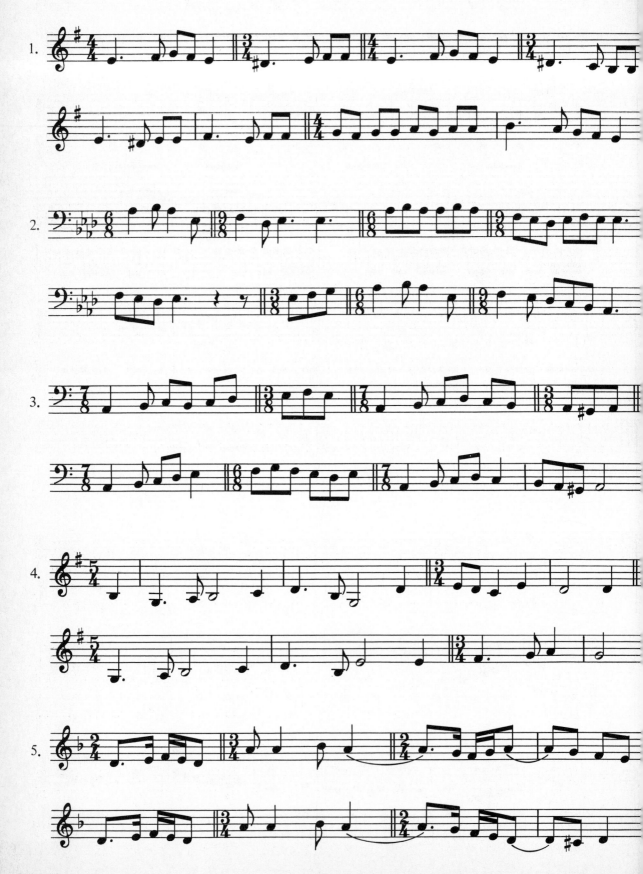

(4) COORDINATED MELODIC-RHYTHMIC EXERCISES

(5) MIXED METERS—CHANGING NOTE VALUES

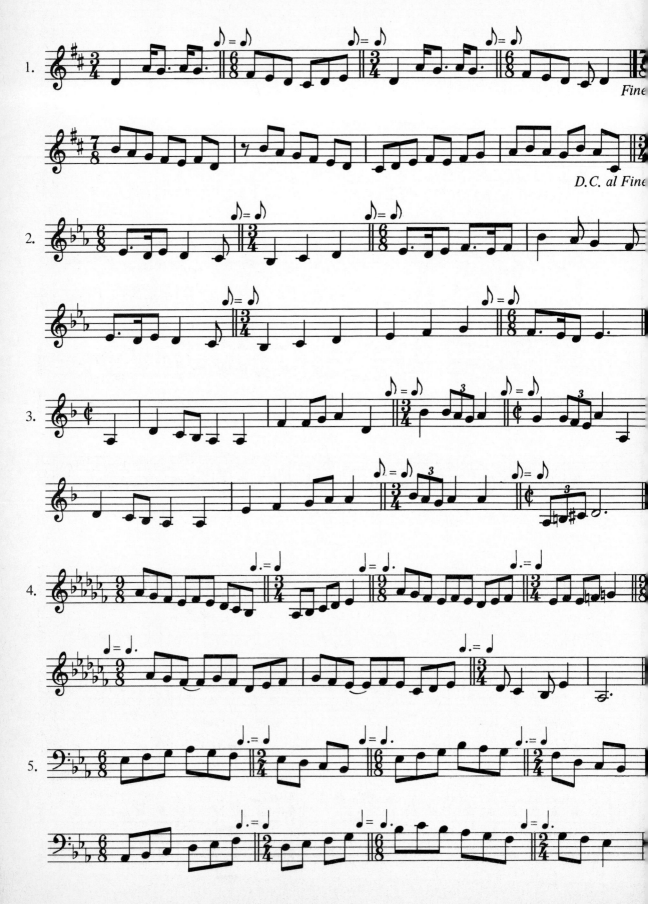

Fine

D.C. al Fine

(7) SYNCOPATION

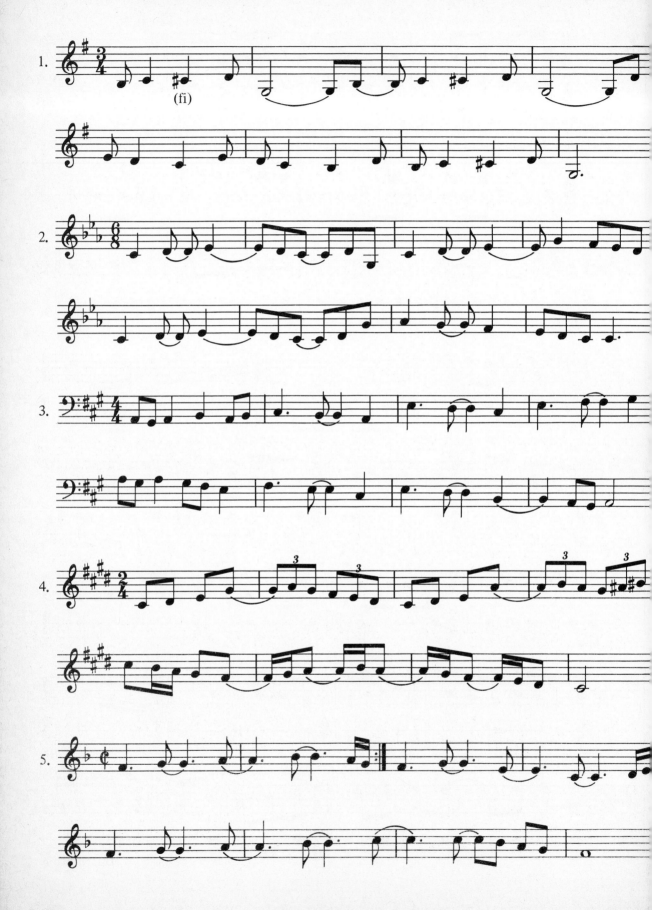

(8) COORDINATED MELODIC-RHYTHMIC EXERCISES

(9) CHURCH MODES AND OTHER SCALE FORMS

The solfeggio system can also be used for sight singing music in the church modes (see 3m). In examples 1–4 below, the syllables indicated are for the movable-*do* system. Since the movable-*do* system implies a tonic, it is impractical for examples 5 and 6, which use the whole-tone and pentatonic scales (see 3n). In singing such examples, where a clear tonality or key center is lacking, the fixed *do* system is useful, or use *la* as a substitute for solfeggio or letter names.

Melodic Writing, Harmonization, and Transposition

8a   **Melodic Writing**

Writing melodies is a goal of most beginning students of music theory. Composing the "great" melody is as much luck as it is a skill, but some very general rules may help you begin this rather personal and complex task. Remember that some of the most memorable melodies are the simplest and direct in form.

1. Melodic lines are divided into "periods," comparable to a sentence of written prose. A completed melody will be made up of several periods, usually of even numbers, 2–4 or 8.

2. A "period" will be four, eight, or possibly 16 measures in length.

3. Each "period" has two "phrases." Phrases are usually structured in a question (antecedent) answer (consequent) format. The first phrase (antecedent) ends on a pitch other than tonic (see 6b) and the second phrase (consequent) ends on the tonic.

4. A period may be parallel in form (first and second phrases are similar) or contrasting in form (first and second phrases are not similar).

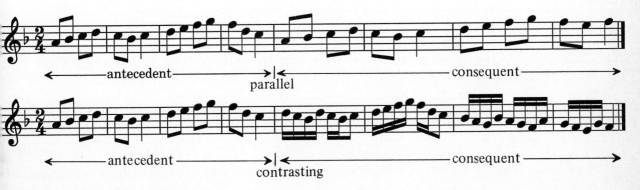

5. A melody is made up of two components—pitch and rhythm. Many times the strength of a melody lies in a repeated rhythmic pattern, or a unique pattern of pitches or intervals, but most often, a combination of both.

Rhythm

Pitch

Combined

6. Melodic lines may move by (a) scale steps with few interval skips, (b) outline chords, (c) wide interval leaps (more instrumental than vocal) or in combination.

(a)

(b)

(c)

7. Ascending musical lines generate more energy and drama, a descending musical line less energy and a sense of repose.

← tension ——————→ | ← relaxation ——————→

Melodic lines have an overall "architecture." The two phrases may remain relatively static, or the first phrase ascends and the second phrase descends, or first descends and then ascends and perhaps both phrases could ascend or descend.

8. The overall range (lowest to highest note) of a melody will be dictated by the instrument or voice for which you are writing. The vocal range (tessitura) of the untrained voice is at maximum approximately an octave and a fifth.

9. To add an accompaniment to a melody, remember that a melodic line will tend to imply chords (see 8b).

8b Harmonization

Adding an accompaniment, or musical background, to a melody is called **harmonization**. Most melodies can be harmonized simply, using only the primary triads I, IV, and V (see 6c). Being able to improvise an accompaniment to a song or folk tune is fun, and you need not be an expert pianist to learn to do it. The following guidelines are very general, but they will help you to establish the key of a melody and to decide which chord or chords you will use in each measure.

1. Establish the key of the melody in any or all of the following three ways:
   a. Look at the key signature.
   b. Look at the first and the last tones of the melody.
   c. See if the implied chords at the beginning of the first full measure and at the end of the last measure are the same. Generally they are, and this chord is the tonic (I).
2. Once you have verified the key, establish the primary chords (I, IV, V, or V_7) in that key.
3. The accompaniment chords should contain the tones found in the melody. Tones on strong beats are more important than tones on weaker beats (see 1f).
4. Some tones in the melody may not belong to the accompaniment chords. These are nonharmonic tones, which are discussed in the following section.

(1) NONHARMONIC TONES

Nonharmonic tones are any tones in a melody that are not included in the underlying chord (or harmony). There are many kinds of nonharmonic tones. Six of the most important are discussed here.

(a) Passing tones

Passing tones occur stepwise between two chord tones. In the examples below, the passing tones are circled. In each case, they "pass" from one tone of the C major triad to another tone of the triad. All the passing tones in these examples are *unaccented* passing tones, since they occur on the weak part of the beat.

Accented passing tones occur on the strong part of the beat, as in the following examples.

(b) Neighboring tones

Neighboring tones, or auxiliary tones, occur stepwise above or below a repeated chord tone. A neighboring tone may be diatonic or chromatic, unaccented or accented. In the following example, (a) shows upper neighboring tones and (b) shows lower neighboring tones. All are unaccented.

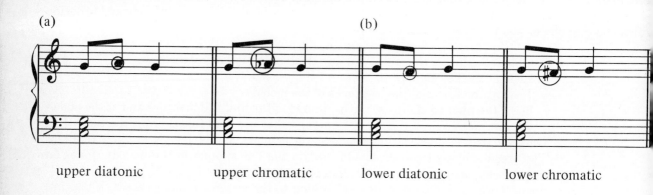

In examples (c) and (d) below, the neighboring tones are accented, occuring on the strong part of the beat.

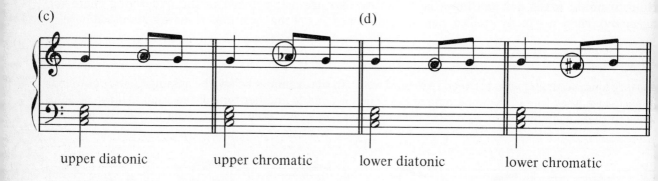

(c) Échappée and cambiata (escape tones)

An *échappée* is a nonharmonic note moving away from two harmonic notes. In contrast, the *cambiata* is a nonharmonic note that moves in the same direction of the harmonic notes.

(d) Appoggiatura

An *appoggiatura* is a nonharmonic note, a second above or below, occurring on a strong beat and resolving to a harmonic note.

(e) Anticipation

An *anticipation* is a nonharmonic note that anticipates a harmonic note of the following chord.

(f) Suspension

A *suspension* is a harmonic note that has been suspended into the following chord and is resolved, stepwise down, to a harmonic note.

(g) Pedal point

A *pedal point* is a note, generally in the bass that is sustained while other parts have changing harmonies.

(2) ADDING AN ACCOMPANIMENT

An accompaniment consisting only of root-position primary chords is dull to listen to and awkward to play. For these reasons, the most common accompaniment progression is root-position tonic, second-inversion subdominant (IV_4^6), and first-inversion dominant seventh (V_5^6). For further ease in performance, the *fifth* of the dominant seventh is usually omitted. This progression is shown below in all major keys, in circle-of-fifths order. (The starred progressions are enharmonic equivalents.) Although the progression is generally played with the left hand, it can readily be played with the right hand if the melody is in the bass. Left-hand fingerings are included in the first example, and the same fingerings should be used in every key.

Practice this pattern until you are comfortable with it in all major keys. You should also practice it throughout the *minor* circle of fifths.

The following two-hand progression is useful in accompanying an instrumental or vocal soloist or group. This progression is shown in all major keys, in circle-of-fifths order. (The starred progressions are enharmonic equivalents.) Practice until you are comfortable in all major keys then also practice it throughout the *minor* circle of fifths.

*enharmonic equivalents

Accompaniment Patterns

The following patterns are just a sampling of the almost endless possibilities for varying the primary chords. Be experimental and devise other patterns; also try using more than one pattern in a single accompaniment. The patterns are written in simple meters, but they are easily adaptable to compound meters.

(1) PATTERNS IN 2/4

(2) PATTERNS IN 3/4

(4) POP PATTERNS

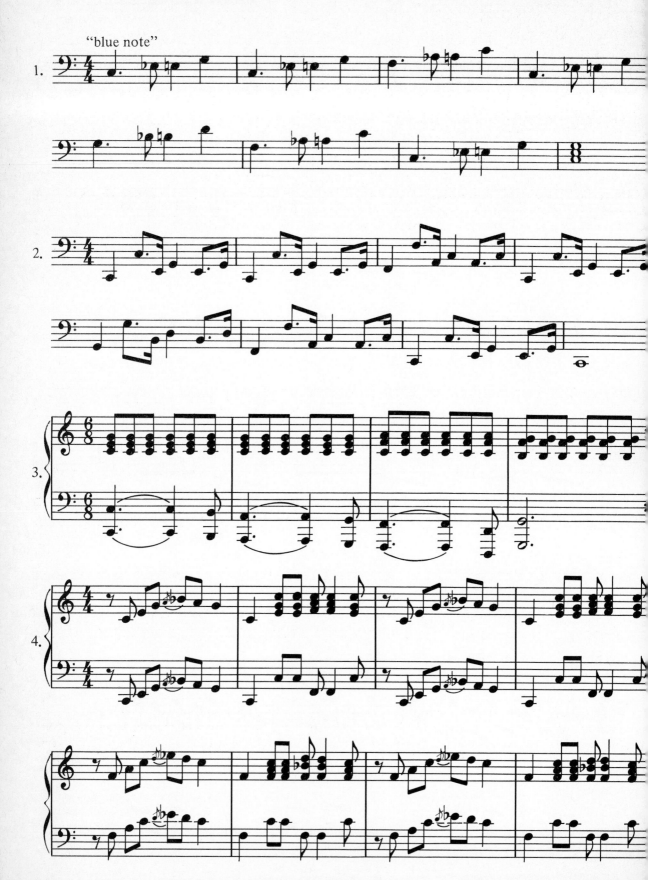

"blue note"

1.

2.

3.

4.

8d   Transposition

To **transpose** a melody or composition is to rewrite or perform it in a different key than the original. Transposition is an essential skill for singers who wish to perform a piece in a more comfortable range, and it is a skill required for accompanists, conductors, composers, and for some instrumentalists.

(1) SHIFTING NOTES ON THE STAFF

There are two methods of transposition. The first, and most common, is the shifting of notes on the staff to the new key. For example, if you wanted to transpose a melody from C to E♭ major (up a minor third), you would write every note up a minor third and add the new key signature (three flats), as in the example below. Note that you could also write every note *down* a major sixth, in accordance with the principles of interval inversion (4h).

MELODY TO BE TRANSPOSED

original key: C

to E♭: up a minor third

to E♭: down a major sixth

It is easy to check your work in this method of transposition by remembering that the movable-*do* solfeggio syllables and the scale-degree numbers of the transposed melody will always be the same as those of the original key. In the example above, the melody begins do-re-mi-re-mi-fa-sol-fa (1-2-3-2-3-4-5-4) in both C and E♭, and in whatever other key you transpose the melody to—*if* you have moved the notes correctly.

261

(2) CHANGING THE CLEF

The second method of transposition is to change the *clef* instead of the notes on the staff. In this method, t•
change a melody, you would simply alter the clef sign and add the new key signature. This method, which
is used in some conservatories, has the advantage of not requiring the complete rewriting of a melody o•
piece, but you must be familiar with all seven clefs (see 1b).

In the following example, a melody is given without clef or key signature. You would decide what rang•
you wish and pick the appropriate clef. For example, if you want the melody in the key of B or B♭ major o•
minor, you would use the tenor clef and add the appropriate key signature. This method is a fairly eas•
skill to develop in strictly diatonic music, but difficult when accidentals (chromaticism) are introduced.

MELODY TO BE TRANSPOSED

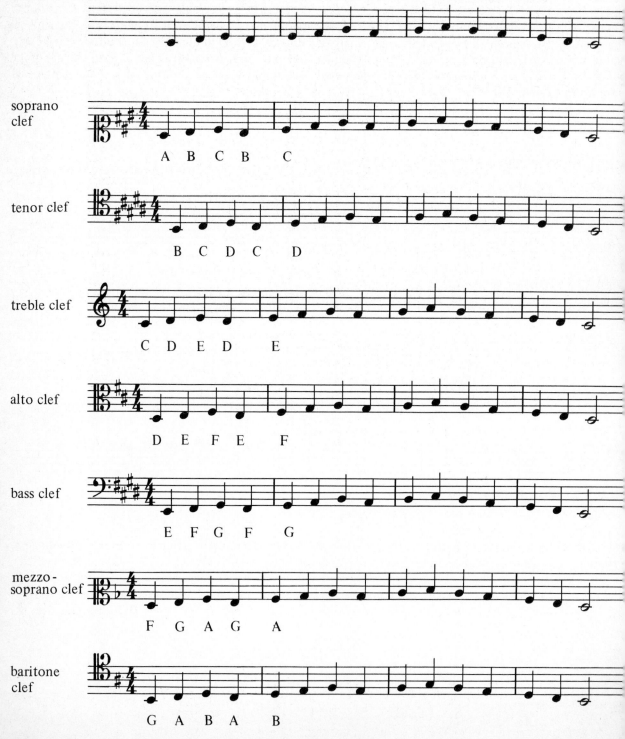

(3) INSTRUMENTAL TRANSPOSITION

here are a number of orchestral instruments that *transpose*. These instruments, for historical and
coustical reasons, were written in keys other than that of their actual sound. The clarinet, French horn,
rumpet, and saxophones are transposing instruments. Their *given key*, based on their individual over-
one series (see 3d), is the pitch they sound if they play the note C. The B♭ clarinet is a B♭ instrument. If the
♭ clarinet plays C it will sound B♭, a Major 2nd *lower*. Therefore, if you write for the B♭ clarinet you must
ranspose *up* a Major 2nd. If the F French horn plays C it will sound F, a Perfect 5th *lower*. Therefore, if you
rite for the F French horn you must transpose *up* a Perfect 5th.

Following is a list of the transposing instruments. For each, the note C is given and the *actual sound* is
lso given.

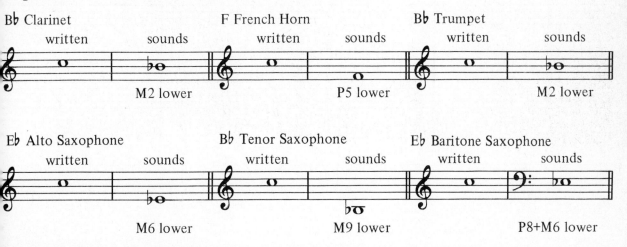

nstruments that sound their actual pitch are non-transposing, *concert-pitched* or C instruments. The
iolin, viola, cello, flute, oboe, bassoon, trombone, and tuba are non-transposing. The piccolo and string
ass are also C instruments. The piccolo sounds one octave higher than written and the string bass sounds
ne octave lower than written.

lease note that the baritone saxophone is a bass instrument but is written in the treble clef. The
axophones are all written in treble clef to allow the performer to play all of the instruments without the
eed of clef changes.

Complete the following periods in *parallel* form.

Complete the following periods in *contrasting* form.

Write an opening phrase for the following periods in *parallel* form.

Write an opening phrase for the following periods in *contrasting* form.

5. Write melodies using the rhythms given.

6. Write a period with the opening phrase (antecedent) *ascending* and the closing phrase (consequent) *descending*.

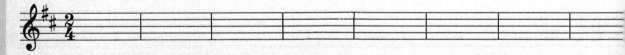

7. Write a period with the opening phrase (antecedent) *descending* and the closing phrase (consequent) *ascending*.

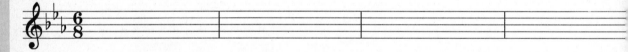

8. Write a period with both phrases ascending.

9. Write a period with both phrases descending.

NAME _____

In the following examples, circle and label nonharmonic tones.

UPT	unaccented passing tone	A	anticipation
APT	accented passing tone	App	appoggiatura
UN	upper neighboring (auxiliary) tone	E	échappée
LN	lower neighboring (auxiliary) tone	C	cambiata
S	suspension		

NAME _____

8b
(1)
(2)

In the following melodies, establish the correct primary chords, circle and label the nonharmonic tones and then write two possible accompaniment patterns.

8c

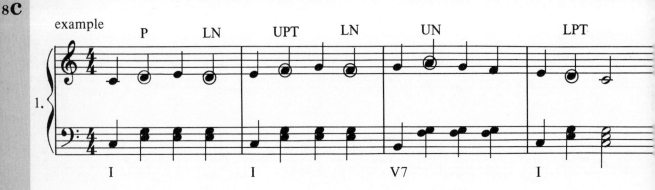

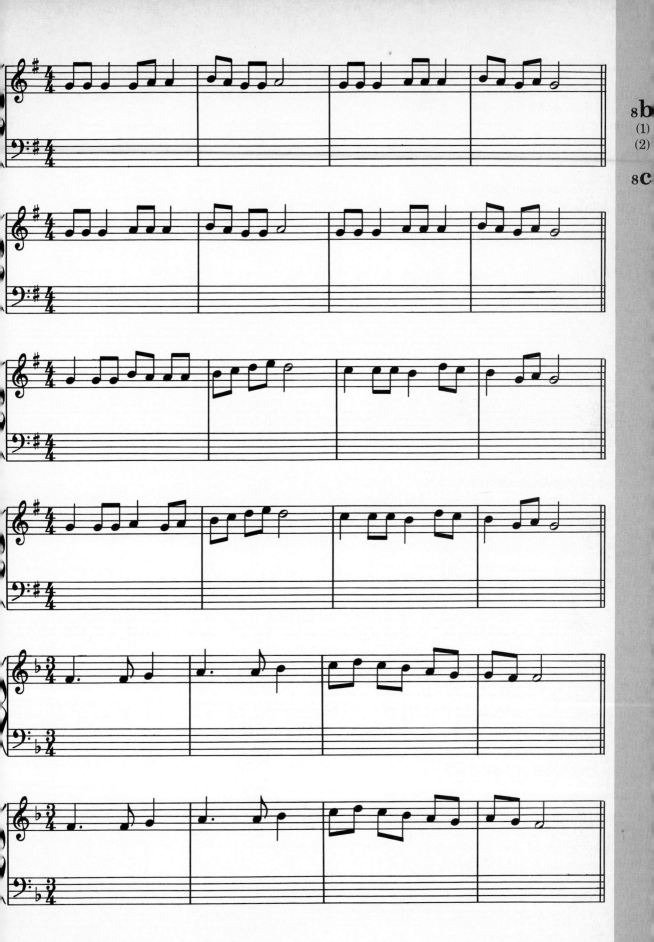

8d
(1)   In the following exercises, establish the new key signature and transpose the notes up or down as indicated

Transpose up from C to E.

1.

Transpose down from C to F.

2.

Transpose up from C to A♭.

3.

Transpose down from C to D.

4.

Transpose up from C to G.

5.

Transpose down from C to B♭.

6.

Transpose up from C to A.

7.

Transpose down from C to E♭.

8.

In the following exercise, establish the new key signature and transpose the notes up or down as indicated.

Transpose up from B♭ to E.

Transpose down from B♭ to F.

Transpose up from B♭ to C.

Transpose down from B♭ to D.

NAME _____

8d
(1)

In the following exercise, establish the new key signature and transpose the notes up or down as indicated

Transpose up from F to G.

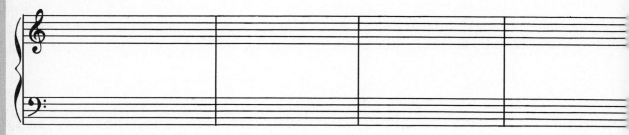

Transpose down from F to B♭.

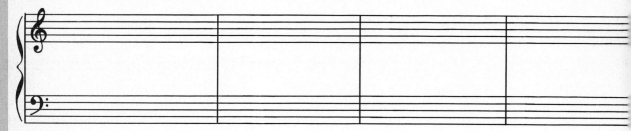

Transpose up from F to A.

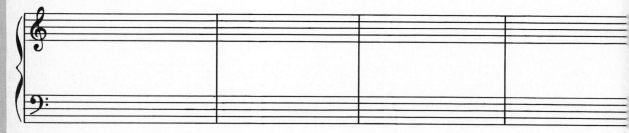

Transpose down from F to E♭.

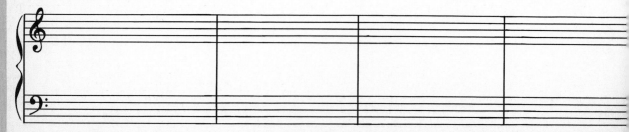

In the following exercises, clefs have been omitted. Using letter names, sing each one in all seven clefs.

Worksheet 8-8

8d
(3)

In the following instrumental transpositions, establish the new key and transpose the notes as required

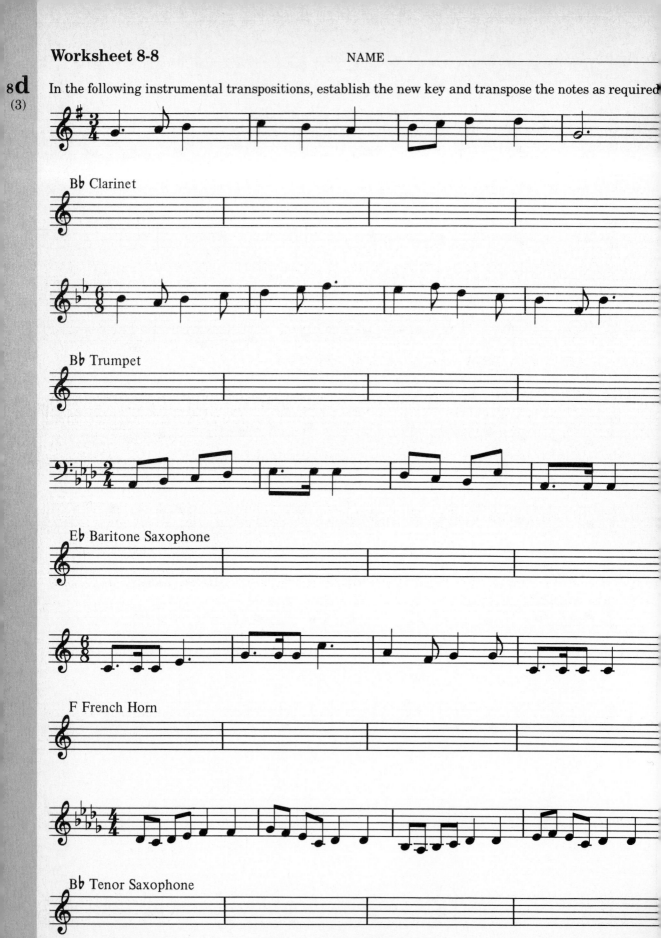

Bb Clarinet

Bb Trumpet

Eb Baritone Saxophone

F French Horn

Bb Tenor Saxophone

Review of Unit 8

8a

1. Write a period in *parallel* form.

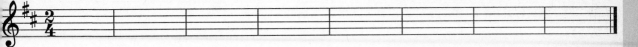

2. Write a period in *contrasting* form.

3. In the following examples circle and label nonharmonic tones.

8b
(1)

4. In the following melodies, establish the correct primary chords, circle and label the nonharmonic tones, and write an accompaniment.

8b
(1)
(2)

8c

5. In the following exercises, establish the new key signature and transpose the notes up or down a
indicated.

Transpose up from G to B♭

Transpose down from g mi to a mi

6. In the following instrumental transpositions, establish the new key and transpose the notes a
required.

E♭ Alto Saxophone

B♭ Trumpet

9

APPENDIX: *Terms, Signs, and Symbols*

The following lists are necessarily not comprehensive. You should consult the Contents for terms and concepts defined and discussed in the text, and one of the standard music dictionaries for other terms, instruments, and symbols not included here.

9a   General Music Terms

a cappella (It., "in chapel style") for unaccompanied voices

Alberti bass a keyboard accompaniment played by the left hand, in which chord tones alternate in a fixed pattern

alla breve (cut time, ₵) simple duple meter with the half note as the beat

anacrusis upbeat

aria song with instrumental accompaniment

arpeggio see Signs and Symbols (9d)

asymmetric meter a meter such as $\frac{5}{8}$ or $\frac{7}{4}$, with unequal division of the measure so that accents occur irregularly

atonal without tonality; not in a key

augmentation increasing, usually doubling, the durational value of a note or passage

authentic cadence the harmonic progression V_7-I used at the end of a phrase or composition

basso continuo same as figured bass (see 6e)

cadence a point of repose at the end of a phrase, section, or composition

cadenza a solo passage in improvisatory style

clavier any keyboard instrument

coda a strongly conclusive final section of a movement or composition; *codetta*: a small coda

common time (C) $\frac{4}{4}$ time

consonance a stable combination of tones that does not require resolution

contrapuntal pertaining to counterpoint

counterpoint music consisting of two or more independent lines

cut time see *alla breve*

deceptive cadence the harmonic progression V-VI (instead of V-I) at the end of a phrase

diatonic a term describing the notes of the major or natural minor scale, excluding all chromatic alterations

diminution decreasing, usually halving, the durational value of a note or passage

dissonance an unstable combination of tones that requires resolution

doppio double

equal temperament a system of tuning in which the octave is divided into twelve equal intervals

grace note see Signs and Symbols (9d)

ground bass a phrase continuously repeated in the bass

half cadence an incomplete cadence, usually on dominant harmony

homophony music in which a melody, usually in the highest voice, is supported by a chordal accompaniment

intonation accuracy of pitch in singing or playing tones

key signature one or more sharps or flats grouped at the beginning of the staff indicating what notes are to be altered throughout the piece

maggiore major

meter signature the two numbers at the beginning of a piece indicating a recurring pattern of accented and unaccented beats. The top number indicates the number of beats grouped into each measure; the bottom number indicates the note value of the beat.

metronome a pendulum device used to determine and regulate tempo

minore minor

mode any scale form; before about 1600, usually one of the church modes; after about 1600, usually major or minor

modulation change of key in the course of a composition

monophony music consisting of a single unaccompanied melody

opus (op.) a musical composition (usually accompanied by a number); the works of a composer are numbered consecutively—op.1, op.2, etc.—in order of composition or publication

ostinato (It., "obstinate") a figure or phrase continuously repeated throughout a passage or composition

ottava (8, 8va) octave

pianoforte the original, unabbreviated name for the piano

pitch a musical sound as measured by how low or high it is within a scale

polychord a combination of two or more different chords

plagal cadence the harmonic progression IV-I (the "amen" cadence)

polyphony see *counterpoint*

polytonality the simultaneous use of two or more tonal centers or keys

prime perfect unison

resolution the progression of a dissonant interval or chord to a consonant (stable) interval or chord

scherzo (It., "joke") a brusque or humorous composition in triple meter; a scherzo is sometimes used in symphonies, sonatas, etc., in place of a minuet

segno sign

sequence the immediate duplication of a tonal pattern in the same part(s) at a different pitch

tempo the rate of speed of a musical composition

thoroughbass same as figured bass (see 6e)

timbre tone color or quality

tone row same as twelve-tone row (see 3p)

9b Performance Terms

accelerando (accel.) increasing in tempo

adagio leisurely, slow; *adagietto*: a little faster than adagio

ad libitum (ad lib.) at will; at the performer's discretion

affrettando (affrett.) hurrying

agitato in an agitated or excited manner

al fine (repeat) to the end

allargando (allarg.) decreasing in tempo

allegro fast; *allegretto*: slightly slower than allegro

all'ottava (8va---) when above the notes: play an octave higher; when below the notes: play an octave lower

andante moderately slow: *andantino*: slightly faster than andante

animato with animation

a piacere at pleasure; without measured tempo

appassionata passionately

arco bow: with the bow

assai very

a tempo return to the first tempo

attacca proceed to the next section or movement without pause

brio fire; vigor

calando (cal.) decreasing in tempo and loudness

cantabile (cantab.), *cantando*, *cantante* in singing style

con with

crescendo (cresc.) increasing in loudness

da capo (D.C.) (repeat) from the beginning

dal segno (D.S.) (repeat) from the sign

decrescendo (decresc.) decreasing in loudness

diminuendo (dim., dimin.) decreasing in loudness

divisi (div.) divided; an indication that a vocal or instrumental section is to divide and perform two or more parts

dolce (dol.) sweetly

doloroso sadly; plaintively

energico with energy

espressivo (espr., espress.) expressively

fermata see Signs and Symbols (9d)

fine the end; the concluding point after a return to the beginning or to a sign

forte (f) loud; *fortissimo* (ff): very loud

forte-piano (fp) loud, then immediately soft

forza fire; forcefulness

giocoso playfully

giusto strict; exact

glissando a sliding-pitch effect

G.P. (grand pause) silence; a rest for the entire orchestra or ensemble

grave slow; solemnly, seriously

grazioso gracefully

hold same as fermata (see Signs and Symbols, 9d)

l'istesso tempo the same tempo

largo broad; very slow; *larghetto*: slightly faster than largo; *larghissimo*: the slowest tempo indication

legato (leg.) very smooth, with no separation between notes (see Signs and Symbols, 9d)

lento slow, but not as slow as largo

loco as written (used after *all'ottava*)

maestoso majestically

marcato (marc.) marked; stressed

marziale martially

meno mosso, meno moto with less movement; slower

mezzo half; moderately

mezzo forte (*mf*) not as loud as forte; *mezzo piano* (*mp*): not as soft as piano

misterioso mysteriously

M.M. (Maelzel metronome) used with a number to indicate tempo; the number indicates beats per minute

moderato moderate (tempo)

molto very

morendo (mor.) dying away; fading

mosso, moto motion

non not

ossia otherwise; indicates another way of performing a passage

pesante (pes.) heavily

piano (*p*) soft; *pianissimo* (*pp*): very soft

più more

più mosso, più moto with more movement; faster

pizzicato (pizz.) plucked (instead of bowed, in string parts)

poco little; a little

presto very fast; *prestissimo*: faster than presto; the fastest tempo indication

quasi in the manner of

rallentando (rall.) gradually slowing

rinforzando (rf., rfz., rinf.) reinforced; suddenly stressed

ritardando (rit., ritard.) gradually slowing

ritenuto holding back; immediately slower

rubato with rhythmic freedom

scherzando playfully

secco dry; drily

segue follows; continues in the same way

sempre (sem., semp.) always; throughout

senza without

sforzando (*sf*, *sfz*) with force; with an explosive accent

simile similarly; in the same way

sordino mute

sostenuto (sost.) sustained

sotto under; below

staccato (stacc.) detached; separated (see Signs and Symbols, 9d)

stringendo (string.) accelerating markedly; hastening

subito suddenly

tacet silent; a part so marked is silent for the entire section or movement

tanto much; so much

tempo I, tempo primo return to the first tempo

tenuto (ten.) held; sustained for full value

tremolo ("trembling") the rapid repetition of one note or the rapid alternation of two notes

troppo too much

una corda (u.c.) a piano indication of the use of the soft pedal

vibrato (vib.) slight fluctuation of pitch or intensity

vivace spirited, lively; *vivacissimo*: very spirited, very lively

vivo lively

Instruments of the Orchestra

English Name	Italian Name	French Name	German Name
Flute	Flauto	Flûte	Flöte
Oboe	Oboe	Hautbois	Oboe (or Hoboe)
Clarinet	Clarinetto	Clarinette	Klarinette
Bassoon	Fagotto	Basson	Fagott
Horn	Corno	Cor	Horn
Trumpet	Tromba	Trompette	Trompete
Trombone	Trombone	Trombone	Posaune
Tuba	Tuba	Tuba	Tuba (or Bass tuba)
Timpani (or kettledrums)	Timpani	Timbales	Pauken
Harp	Arpa	Harpe	Harfe
Violin	Violino	Violon	Geige (or Violine)
Viola	Viola	Alto	Bratsche (or Viole)
Violoncello (or cello)	Violoncello	Violoncelle	Violoncello
Double Bass (or contrabass)	Contrabasso	Contrebasse	Kontrabass

9d # Signs and Symbols

accent   >or -   either mark, placed above or below a note, indicates that emphasis should be added to the affected note.

legato slur   a curved line placed over or under several different notes. The slur indicates that the notes should be played very smoothly. Legato is the opposite of staccato (see below).

staccato dot   a dot placed above or below a note. Staccato dots indicate that the affected note should be shortened and detached from the other notes.

appoggiatura		a nonharmonic, ornamental tone that precedes a chord tone. Unlike the grace note (see below), the appoggiatura is subject to a strict beat.

sounds

grace note		a nonharmonic, ornamental tone that precedes a chord tone. The grace note is not subject to a strict beat.

sounds

breath mark	**'**	indicates that the notes should be separated, as if for a breath.

arpeggio		the wavy line indicates that the notes should be played from bottom to top in rapid succession.

measured		a single slash above or below a note indicates a subdivision into eighth notes; a double slash indicates sixteenth notes; and a triple slash indicates either thirty-second notes or that the tremolo should be played as fast as possible.

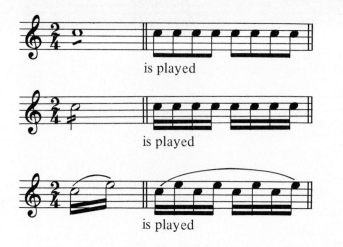

trill	*tr*	the abbreviation *tr*, with or without a wavy line following it, indicates a rapid alternation with the diatonic second (or chromatic second if an accidental is included) above a written note. Performance practices and styles vary, but in general, 17th- and 18th-century trills begin on the diatonic step above and the modern trill begins with the note indicated.

fermata		indicates that a note should be held for longer than its normal value.

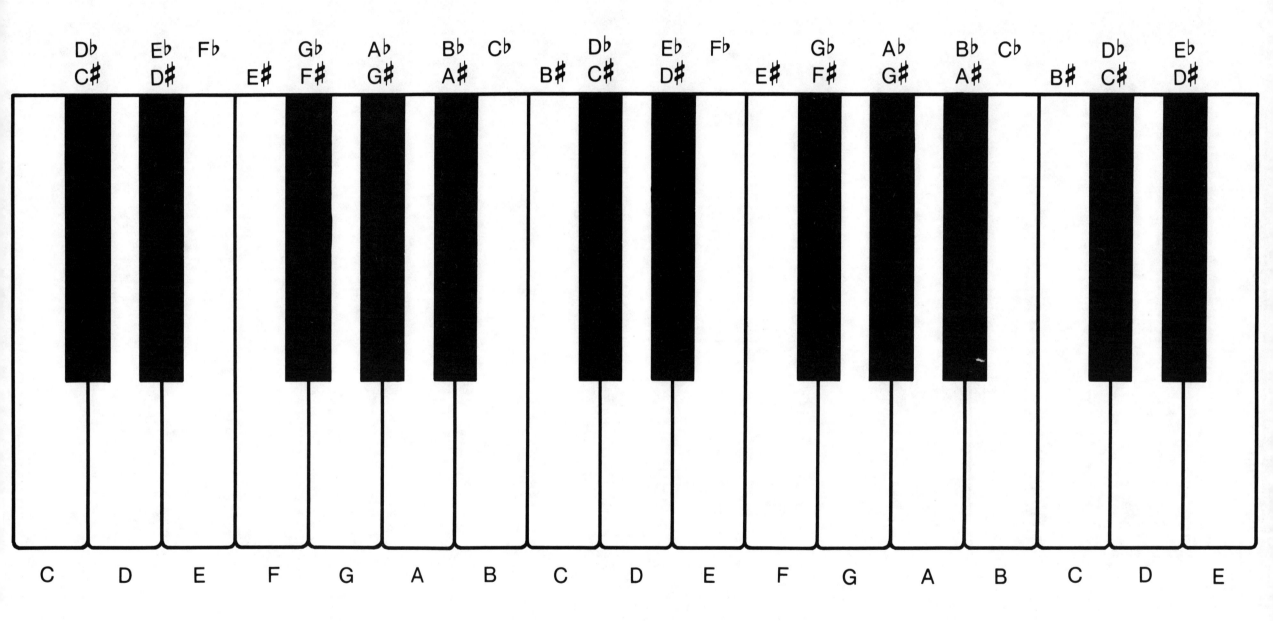